CHRYSLER MUSCLE

Detroit's Mightiest Machines

Bill Holder and Phil Kunz

Published by

700 East State Street • Iola, WI 54990-0001
715-445-2214 • 888-457-2873
www.krause.com

Please call or write for our free catalog of publications.
Our toll-free number to place an order or obtain a free catalog is 800-258-0929 or please use our regular business telephone 715-445-2214 for editorial comments and further information.

ISBN: 0-87349-633-7
Library of Congress Catalog Number: 2003108883
Printed in the United States of America

Edited by: Tom Collins
Designed by: Brian Brogaard

ACKNOWLEDGMENTS

Thanks to the following Mopar car owners for letting us photograph their beautiful vehicles:

Mike Alexander
John Balow
John Barnes
Larry Bell
Earl Brown
Tom Brown
David Clabuesch
Fred Englehart
Chet Gibbs
Leroy Hopkinds
John Johnson
Tom Kroner
Paul Lepart
Chris Levering
Bob and Sharon
Malcom
Phil McEldownievers
Bob Morgan
Ken Mosier
Bobby and Linda
Newman
Very Peine
Mike Penland
Gary Plessenger
Jody Reasoner
Scott Reasoner
Steve Russell
Michael Smith
Mike and Vicky
Sylvester
Richard Speakman
Steve Tiemeier
Tom Veach
Bill Werner
James Whipple
Ron Wietholter
Randall Waring

Technical assistance from:

Mike Alexander
Steve Atwell
John Balow
John Barnes
Larry Bell
Earl Brown
John Carollo
David Clabuesch
Tony Depillo
Fred Englehart
Ed and Sue George
Jeff Johnson
John Johnson
T.E. McHale
Bob Morman
John Murphy
Mike and Vicky
Sylvester
James Whipple
Randall Waring

CONTENTS

T/A
340 SIX PAK
T/A
340 SIX PAK
GOODYEAR
EAGLE GT

FOREWORD

I got to know Bill Holder first over the telephone. As incoming editor of Dobb's Publishing's *Musclecar Review* magazine, I inherited a network of first-class freelance contributors, including Bill who was one of the most prolific.

Standard procedure for getting a freelance story published is for the freelancer to find a great car, pitch the story to the editor, then—if the editor bites—photograph it and write the copy.

As Bill would call with his latest finds, I could hear a genuine passion for the classic muscle cars through the telephone. There was no mistaking the enthusiasm as Bill would describe a certain car that got him all revved up. He would tell me about its spectacular color, high-powered engine, and driveline options in tones reminiscent of a kid who'd just come from a big-league baseball game after snagging a home run.

After years in any business things can become routine, but Bill never lost his deep appreciation for this incomparable generation of American classics. Chrysler built plenty of muscle cars that make it easy to get excited about.

No manufacturer was more outrageous in engineering and style. Who else could have created the Road Runner? The Cross Ram 413? The Pistol Grip and Slap Stick shifters? The winged Daytona and Superbird? Pulling their punches just wasn't what the good folks at Chrysler were all about. And that kind of passion fuels more passion. No brand of muscle car has a more devoted following.

Ever been to the Mopar Nationals? It's a wild weekend that has no equal. It's where well-heeled collectors of high-buck Hemi 'Cudas enjoy a natural fellowship with T-shirted college kids in a beater four-door Coronet. Where guys book the same week of vacation every year, stay up most of the night bench-racing with friends in the hotel parking lot, yet rise early to get out to the track before 8 a.m. the next morning.

Mopar also has its own distinctive culture, with its own dialect (Sure Grip, Track Pack, B5, F8, etc.), art (Peter Max-esque psychedelic ads from the late 1960s) and holidays (Mopar Nationals, virtually any NHRA event where the Hemi design rules).

And who better to examine this topic than Bill Holder? Fifteen years later, when Bill calls to pitch me a story for my new magazine, *Musclecar Power*, I can still hear the excitement in his voice. Bill truly appreciates the cars and culture, and sees his work through the eyes of a genuine enthusiast. I find working with Bill to be just as rewarding as ever. If you count yourself as one of the Mopar Faithful, this book should be a blast.

—Tom Shaw, publisher
Musclecar Power magazine
P.O. Box 6085
Lakeland, FL 33807
www.musclecarpower.com

INTRODUCTION

The Muscle Car Magic from Chrysler

Pizzazz! Style! Outrageous! Macho! Powerful! They had it all. Chrysler Corporation's Dodge and Plymouth lines of the late 1960s and early ´70s (just about a decade in all) brought forth a multitude of new moods and new ways of thinking about these new lines of Chrysler machines.

It was an era the U.S. automotive industry had never seen before, and probably will never see again. It became known as the muscle car era, and Chrysler used this special period to perfection as it marketed its new sexy look and "mod" style.

The styling and detailing was ageless. Chrysler's muscle cars look just as good many decades later. And they are memorable—definitely not the cookie-cutter designs of today.

With the blunt front-end designs most of these models possessed, there certainly was no consideration of aerodynamics.

But aerodynamics alone can create bland designs and no Chrysler muscle car could be

Unique performance-oriented detailing, like this ´71 ´Cuda, was the rage in Mopar's late-´60s and early ´70s models.

The era of style and performance was typified by this ´69 Charger R/T. Many buyers emphasized the muscle look with small wheelcovers.

identified as bland! Each of the Dodge and Plymouth models of this era had its own personality.

They were designed to leave an impression not to slide through the air. Chrysler muscle cars just looked good!

Even with many models sharing the same body basics, each of these memorable models stood out with its own indelible image.

Chrysler Corporation employed some amazing, street-smart techniques with the public hoping to achieve success in dealer showrooms. Using a hip national advertising campaign—the race-inspired designs, high-performance power plants, targeted to youth and often featuring knock-out "Valley Girl" models, Chrysler's national advertising stirred the testosterone levels of young males and made innovative use of coloring, detailing, and graphics. It all was focused on these modern street machines. Chrysler's muscle cars grabbed the attention of the automotive experts and the general public's interest in their products also was sky-high. And their nickname came from the parts and performance arm of Chrysler—Mopar.

For the most part, today's youth have no idea what they´re looking at when they view one of these out-of-sight 1960s-´70s car creations. They just can't believe the eye-popping beauty is all original and came that way from the factory. In every respect they have an aftermarket look.

It's interesting that the two distinct brands, Dodge and Plymouth, actually carried this revolutionary car culture concept with each division doing its darndest to keep its name out front. Despite those efforts, people didn't use or remember the Dodge or Plymouth monikers but they sure remembered the model names, whether it was the Charger, Challenger or Dart from the "Dodge Rebellion," or the GTX, ´Cuda and Road Runner from the heartbeat of Plymouth.

It was one of the greatest trips in performance car history. Come along for the ride!

The popularity of the Barracuda caused Plymouth to use its ´Cuda nickname. It stuck with fans and still is revered today.

The magnificent 426 Hemi power plant was a star performer. It was an icon then and is highly collectable today.

One glance tells everyone watching this 1971 Plymouth Road Runner is a Chrysler-built muscle car.

Those outlandish colors! They're typified by the Lime Green metallic '70 'Cuda. The rainbow of Chrysler colors stood out!

Chapter One: The Heritage of Power and Performance

The swept-back roofline of a Dodge Charger. The unique profile of Plymouth Barracuda. The distinctive "beep-beep" of the Plymouth Road Runner's horn. The rumble of a Hemi-powered Dodge Coronet at idle. Dodge and Plymouth muscle cars—the Mighty Mopars—were memorable.

While fans of each of the Dodge and Plymouth models swore their favorite designs were totally unique, that wasn't exactly the case. The basic sheet metal was shared in similar models for both brands.

For example, the Dodge Super Bee and Plymouth Road Runner had identical bodies. The differences were in the way they were detailed, chromed, and advertised. Often, added differences made it difficult to recognize their common body shapes.

To keep things interesting, Chrysler Corporation used color, nomenclature, and detailing to differentiate between the identical engines used in Dodge and Plymouth models.

One example is the triple-carbed induction system. It was popular with the 340- and 440-cid power plants, and was called the "Six-Pack" with Dodge versions while Plymouth used "Six-Barrel" with their models.

There was another language used by the ardent fans of these cars. You still might overhear discussions about "A" and "B" bodies at car shows today. Here's what it all means.

The "A" body designation identified the smaller-bodied machines that included the Dodge Dart and Demon and Plymouth's Duster.

The larger "B" body classification included Plymouth's GTX, Satellite, and Road Runner. The Super Bee, Charger, and Coronet were the "B"-bodied Dodge models.

Interestingly, the lettered-body vehicles were produced in the same factories, even though the end products were Plymouth or Dodge products. Their factory assembly proximity was the closest these lines would ever be. Once ready for delivery, they went their

The mid-1950s saw NASCAR dominated by Chrysler 300s powered by early-versions of Hemi powerplants.

own Plymouth and Dodge directions, each taking on their own personalities and loyal fans. All part of Mopar madness!

Today, it's not surprising that the popularity of these models makes these cars prime candidates for fakery. You can believe if you placed a 425-hp Hemi in a 1960s Road Runner that originally came with a 318-cid, the altered car would be worth more—much, much more! Experts could change everything to make less valuable model one appear to be identical to more valuable and original model two.

Often, it comes down to agreeing exactly with what a bogus VIN identification tag would indicate. (And in the Mopar muscle car era, important information tags were found on the inner front fenders and engine blocks as well.)

The allure of these Chrysler muscle products continues to be strong. Be very careful that you are getting what you pay for when you buy one of these performance-oriented classics. Phonies are out there.

An old automotive saying: "Win on Sunday, sell on Monday" was really in vogue during this period. Believe me, the race-prepared versions of a number of these models got it done big time in NASCAR competition!

Three models were built specifically with NASCAR in mind—the 1969 Dodge Charger 500, the 1970 Dodge Charger Daytona, and the 1970 Plymouth Road Runner Superbird. A relatively small number of street versions had to be built in order to qualify for NASCAR participation.

For example, in 1969, Chrysler subcontractor Creative Industries turned out 500 Dodge Charger Daytonas. In 1970, they turned to building even more Plymouth Road Runner Superbird editions for public

The Hemi appeared in other forms during the 1950s. Here, in a DeSoto, it was called the Fire Dome Eight.

Perhaps the ultimate Mopar performance machines were the winged cars, like this Plymouth Road Runner Superbird.

The 1960 Chrysler 300-F was powered by a 413 Wedge power plant capable of 375 hp. Notice the long-tube induction system.

In 1962, the Chrysler 300-H again showed big performance with this twin-carbed power plant capable of 300 horses.

The carbs were staggered atop the 426 Ramcharger power plant during the early 1960s.

consumption. That year, NASCAR required Chrysler and other manufacturers to build one of their specially prepared models per dealer.

Over a decade before, in the mid-1950s, a team of early Hemi-powered Chrysler 300s blew away the

This ´63 Dodge 440 carried the 426 Max Wedge engine—pure drag power! It was "sold as is, no warranty." In 1964, these cars could be purchased with both the 426 Wedge and Hemi engines.

competition. Chrysler's large horsepower offerings started with performance models like the Chrysler C-300, which debuted in 1955. The Chrysler 300 "letter" models brought a new image of raw power to American streets and race tracks, especially with the 355-hp V-8 in the 1956 Chrysler 300-B. Dodge, Plymouth, and DeSoto models all featured powerful V-8s in 1956 and beyond.

It's interesting to note the Chrysler C-300 has been coined the "first American muscle car."

Chrysler products had made an impact on the burgeoning NASCAR tracks of the 1950s. And they joined the growing popularity of drag racing in the early 1960s. Involvement brought more publicity for Chrysler and other manufacturers.

Dodges or Plymouths were the choices of famous drag racing teams of the time including Dick Landy, and Sox and Martin. The Ramchargers were a famous team that included moonlighting Chrysler Corporation employees.

Crossing the finish line in a Chrysler stock car or Hemi-powered dragster kept Chrysler-based products on top. It helped focus on their cars, and especially their power plants made in this period.

By 1960, the new 413-cid Wedge V-8 was capable of producing 400 hp. That engine, used in various model lines, along with the 426 Max Wedge engines introduced in 1962, showed well on the drag strips across America in the early 1960s.

Chrysler Corporation helped the professional teams by building lightweight Super Stock cars that went to a number of professional teams.

Interestingly, Chrysler flaunted the displacement of their potent power plants. For example, a muscular Mopar model of the Plymouth Duster was called the Duster 340, derived from its 340-cid V-8.

You'd better believe that every Dodge fan in North America knew exactly what those numbers stood for! The allegiance to Mopar muscle extended offshore with Chrysler's internationally famous Hemi six-cylinder, originally developed but never used as a domestic truck engine.

A powerful model in Australia and New Zealand was called the Hemi 245. It resembled the North American Dodge Dart. And another North American Dodge model was rebadged the Chrysler 383 in the South Africa market.

It really wasn't necessary to mention the displacement of the awesome 426-cid Hemi V-8. It quickly succeeded in drag and oval-track stock car racing. Everyone knew it as a Hemi.

This '62 Dodge carries the 413 Ramcharger power plant. It definitely was a wolf in sheep's clothing.

Chrysler Corporation realized they could capitalize by using the Hemi name as a prefix, resulting, for example, in the Hemi Challenger or the earlier Plymouth Satellite "Street Hemi" and "Hemi Coronet" models, among others.

If those Chrysler differences weren't enough, what immediately grabbed the public was the number of dazzling new colors that hit the market. Again, they were made on the same assembly lines using the same paint sources for both Dodge and Plymouth. On many occasions, Dodge or Plymouth gave the same color its own unique names, depending on the models.

By the way, these garish colors, or for that matter, any colors that were used, were carried through to the engine compartment and trunk.

The detailing that came with these Dodge and Plymouth models had a number of different motivations, and resulted in a number of memorable enhancements.

Flat black was used to great effect for body striping, hoods, grilles, decals, body lettering, and rear-end valances. White also came into its own in similar, dramatic fashion.

The popular engines themselves received interesting detailing, including a liberal dose of chrome. Hemi Orange was a predominant color on the block and valve

Colors and detailing of the '60s/'70s Mopars have kept them in the 'classic' category four decades later.

covers.

The dazzling striping extended offshore to Chrysler products like the Dodge Dart-based Chrysler Pacers and Chargers built in Australia and New Zealand. They showed considerable pizzazz with striping, blackout grilles, decorated hoods, and more.

The Argentinean, Brazilian, Australian, and New Zealand-built Chrysler products all used distinctive colors and detailing to resemble their famous American Chrysler muscle car counterparts, though their sheet metal "skin" was different.

The engines were smaller in the Aussie, Kiwi, and South American versions, but there was no doubt they had the "tough stuff" of their American cousins.

Unfortunately, like any great dream, you have to wake up sometime and realize the picture your mind painted is over. For the "muscle car era," that happened in the early 1970s with some companies bailing out earlier than others. Chrysler was one of the last to concede that the era was over.

There were many changes. Included were government-mandated emission controls, escalating insurance costs and the rising costs of fuel by 1973. All predicted the end for the Mopar and other muscle car versions.

Changes also affected performance with a lowering of the compression ratio by two full points. Various changes took the heart and soul out of the big block mills. The powerful engines also were hurt by the requirement to begin stating engine horsepower in net form. It was measured with the engine running and all accessories operating and produced a lower equivalent figure.

But even with "muscle cars" waning in popularity, the post-1972 Chrysler versions still retained their macho looks. Some models still were produced until close to the end of the decade. It's interesting that when net horsepower figures started to be used, the promotion of engine displacement numbers was pretty much abandoned.

The Dodge and Plymouth lines reportedly had earlier intentions of continuing the design trends of the late-1960s and early ´70s well into the decade. Some prototype photos from that period point to future production possibilities.

While Chrysler eventually stopped production of their proud Mopar muscle cars, their image never stopped grabbing public attention. In the 2000s, the value of these macho and muscular Chrysler products is unbelievable.

At a January 2002 auction, a Hemi-powered ´69 Plymouth Road Runner with a four-speed transmission reached a top bid of $135,000. The owner turned it down! He thought he could get more if he waited.

Although this glorious era ended over three decades ago, the yearning for those cars continues as strong as ever. Huge national meets still highlight the cars. Die cast models continue to sell. And both stock and modified Dodge and Plymouth configurations roar down drag strips across the country.

Truly, there is nothing like a vintage, muscle-laden Chrysler machine.

The final disposition of the Hemi applied to Mopar muscle machines of the late ´60s and early ´70s, as recognized on the rear flank of the ´70 ´Cuda.

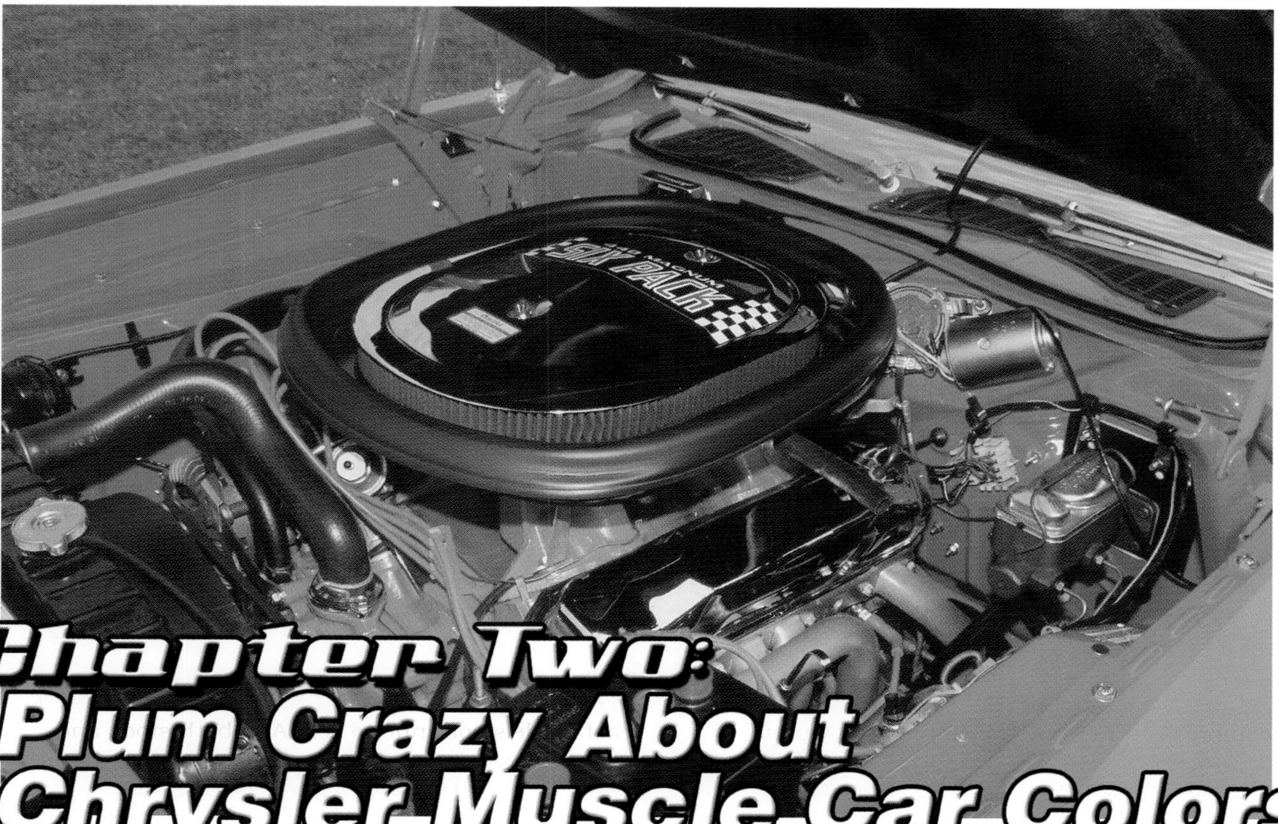

Chapter Two: Plum Crazy About Chrysler Muscle Car Colors

The Dodge and Plymouth lines of the "muscle car" era had much going for them with these sleek, powerful, and beautiful machines. Possibly the first aspect of these cars to hit the senses were the unbelievable colors—an overwhelming feast for the eyes of the era.

Garish had never been the Chrysler image in previous years. Chrysler vehicles were practical, sedate, conservative and projected that image in preceding years, but changes in the "muscle car" era set the buying public on its ear.

Definitely, the youth market was the target for these psychedelic colors. They weren't for everybody—possibly some, but not all of the older generation. For those in their 20s and 30s, the color schemes fit right in with tie-die fashion colors, record album covers and concert posters that were in vogue.

Both divisions turned to bright hues, using some of the same colors, but having some that were unique to their particular brand. Interestingly, when the same color was used by both Mopar divisions, each gave it a different name. That was in keeping with the goal to

Chrysler's FY1 color code was called 'Top Banana' on this 1970 Plymouth Hemi Cuda.

Dodge's version of the FY1 paint code was called 'Lemon Twist' as it appeared on this '70 Challenger R/T.

keep Plymouth and Dodge looking totally separate and holding their particular fans.

For example, Dodge's Copper Metallic was identical to Plymouth's Bronze Fire Metallic. You wouldn't get that idea from those totally different names, but they shared the same color source.

Color names often were as interesting as the colors themselves, reflecting the atmosphere of the country during the late 1960s and early ´70s. There were different names for the same color.

Try Plymouth Lime Light and Dodge Sublime (with the same FJ5 coding) or Plymouth's Top Banana and Dodge's Lemon Twist (FY1). Plymouth had Blue Fire Metallic while Dodge called it Bright Blue Metallic (both B5). Plymouth's In Violet was Dodge's Plum Crazy (both FC7).

This 1970 ´Cuda shines in what Plymouth called 'Sublime.'

Once again, it was a matter of trying to have as much individuality as possible. And both lines were following the Chrysler marketing direction during this wild, golden era in performance auto history.

There were situations when both brands used the same color under the same name. For example, in 1968 Avocado Green Metallic was used by both Dodge and Plymouth with both lines using the same TT1 code.

At other times, the same color would have a different name from one model year to the next. For example, PP1 was Bright Red in Plymouth's 1968 color scheme but carried a new name—Matador Red—for the same coded color the following year.

One of the most popular colors of this era was the Dodge Hemi Orange shade which derived its top-gun Chrysler power plant of the same name. Hemi Orange also was a shade that was used on a number of power plants during the "muscle car" period. Most people wouldn't recognize the name that Plymouth used for that same EV-2 color, Tor-Red, since it definitely was an orange shade!

The color code designations are hard to figure. A large number of the codes, which were used throughout the period, consisted of two letters and a single number—such as TT1, GB5, LL1, etc. In 1969, a single

The Challenger T/A comes at you in what Dodge called 'Limelight' in 1970. Plymouth and Dodge shared Chrysler's FJ5 paint code.

letter was used with a single number—Q5, F8, etc.

There also were some colors in the 1966 and ´67 time period that used three-digit numbers such as 661, 221, and 881.

Many of the models used blackout panels, hoods, rear valances and more to highlight the model's base color. No matter which of the dynamite colors were used, that black association really seems to bring out the particular color.

The wilder colors started to appear in 1968 and lasted through the early-to-mid 1970s. They have survived time and trends, and many of those bright colors still shine in the 21st century, especially in the eyes of Mopar lovers.

A number of the remaining cars have been repainted in the identical factory shade, or at least close to it, but with modern base-coat and clear-coat paint. Those vintage shades still are there, and looking good!

An interesting dealer program took place with a group of 50 1968 Dodge Chargers. Cincinnati had just

You wouldn't expect to see the Sublime body color of this ´70 Plymouth ´Cuda transplanted into the engine compartment, but that's exactly the case here.

The 1970 ´Cuda is painted in what Plymouth called 'In Violet.'

The 1970 Dart is painted in the same color, which Dodge called 'Plum Crazy.' Both cars used Chrysler's FC7 paint code.

Characteristic of Chrysler-built muscle cars was that each body color was used inside the trunk, like this ´74 Road Runner.

been awarded an American Football League (AFL) franchise and a local Dodge dealer decided to celebrate the occasion by creating the "Bengal Charger" model. He used a color very close to Hemi Orange to try to duplicate the orange in the Bengals´ uniform. The design was completed with black bumblebee stripes.

The special Charger carried a black vinyl top and a "Bengal Charger" emblem. A great-looking remembrance of the A.F.L., the early Bengals and the "muscle car" era, but only three are known to remain.

Two years later, a small number of ´70 Barracudas were custom-painted to honor the National Hockey League's St. Louis Blues. They were white coupes with a blue roof and the team's famous "blue note" logo on each door. Only a small number are known to remain.

In order to derive a muscular look, many owners used the small wheel covers. They allowed the body color of the wheels to show, giving the model a drag machine look.

That's not the only part of these cars where the body color continued beyond the external sheet metal. It's amazing, but true, the engine compartments and even the trunks sported the outside color. It produced some interesting color combinations when the hood was raised giving the compartment—with its highly-detailed engine—the look of a modern street machine.

It's interesting how these cars are brought back to life in today's restoration hobby. Some Chrysler muscle enthusiasts try to totally recreate these machines in show car condition. Everything is perfect without a single paint flaw existing. That's not the way they were when they sat in a dealer's showroom.

Rather than wanting their favorite Mopars to have the show car look, they wanted their car exactly the way it came from the production line. Like other mass production cars of the era, that means a certain lack of perfection in these models—such as paint over spray. Many Chrysler muscle car lovers reproduce that phenomenon in their finished products. Originality is everything with some restorers.

And when the vintage Chrysler fans compete in the national meets, stand back when the judging takes place. Probably more than the fans of the other Big-Three brands, these Chrysler muscle car followers are fanatics about color correctness. This writer once saw a huge argument about the exact color shade for a particular model.

Vintage Mopar muscle car fans are an avid group!

During the muscle car era, Plymouth also introduced its so-called "Mod Top".

Chapter Three: Morse Code, Stripes, & More — A Detailed Look

The magnificent colors displayed during this time period were spectacular, but the Dodge and Plymouth Divisions went a little further by setting off those great shades with some out-of-sight detailing.

It was done a number of ways. Detailing included a great collection of clever names, stunning wheel designs, plus the use of black and white stripes on hoods, spoilers, grille treatments, and engines. There were some other colors for miscellaneous uses, plus aggressive detailing of the interiors. The Chrysler stylists seemed to be able to achieve looks that set off each model's base color.

Detailing—Model/Engine Names

Engine and model names were detailed in interesting ways through the wonderful Mopars muscle car years. Not surprisingly, the legendary Hemi engine was rewarded with prominence—initially receiving a chrome tag, with recessed black lettering. The ´69 Hemi Charger R/T received such an emblem.

Use of black backgrounds often was the popular detailing device on sheet metal. When a Hemi engine

This unique wheel was one of many during the Mopar muscle era. Note the blackout portion in the center of the wheel.

was used on Plymouth's ´68 GTX, the name was done in chrome with a black background. A similar treatment was used for the 440 engine. With the ´Cuda, the engine displacement was painted as part of the rear-quarter stripe. Black was the predominant color. The ultimate naming technique used the large side boards which carried the engine identification just past the door handle.

Red was another color used in naming engines and models. Certain 1969 Dodge Dart models featured the '340' number in red. Models with the 340-cid four-barrel or 440-cid six-barrel engine announced the awesome power plant either totally, or partly, in red. The ´70 ´Cuda and Challenger R/T were two examples of this detailing technique.

Detailing-Wheels

The wheels that came with this golden performance and appearance era were up to the rest of the car designs. A number of race- and rod-looking wheels definitely fit the overall aura of the cars!

The most common, and one of the most popular, was the so-called Magnum 500 wheel which appeared on a number of models. The design featured five chrome spokes around a hub with five chrome lug bolts located close to the hub. Between the spokes, was a black background. The wheels usually found themselves as a part of Road Runner, GTX, Charger, and other performance models' exterior appearances.

One of the least common wheels was built for the Charger Daytona. The wheel experienced structural problems and was recalled. A number of the W23 Kelsey-Hayes slotted wheels are still around and are considered a highly-desirable addition to a vintage Chrysler muscle machine.

A ´72 Road Runner GTX sports a classy, slotted and cone-shaped center. Note the light backing surrounding the lug nuts.

Another version of the spinner wheel cover design includes a black-out behind the spinner, demonstrated on this ´66 Charger.

Dodge's Dart family used a similar wheel design. It carried a larger center hub, again with a black background.

The beautiful Rallye Wheel was a choice of many buyers, and was used on Chargers, Challengers, and other models.

But not all of the muscular Chrysler models used

The ´69 Dart GTS was another user of the Rallye Wheel design.

An association with Cragar during this time showcased the classic Cragar Mag in advertising and on beautiful Mopar models.

The attractive Rallye Wheel was available on the Daytona and numerous other Mopar models.

A ´69 Daytona sports the ultra-rare Kelsey-Hayes slotted wheels—recalled shortly after they were issued.

One of a number of wheel covers used was a knock-off spinner design, shown here on a pretty 1965 Plymouth Satellite convertible.

The Rallye Wheel was a popular design carried out here on a ´70 Challenger.

Possibly the most-popular wheel used on the Chrysler-built muscle cars of this era was this five-spoked Magnum 500 wheel.

purely integral wheels. Instead, wheel covers also were used, especially on the earlier models. For example, mid-´60s Plymouth Satellites and Dodge Chargers used similar "spinner hub wheel covers" according to their advertising. Also, there were the small, "dog dish" hub caps that gave each model a completely-new look.

During the muscle car era, Chrysler Corporation had an interesting association with Cragar Industries.

Several small hub cap designs attempted to enhance the drag racing look, typified by this ´68 Charger R/T.

In fact, the companies jointly advertised Cragar's sporty, spoked mag wheels mounted on a ´68 Dodge Charger and a ´69 Dart Swinger. These and other after-market wheels became popular for the performance-oriented Mopars from Dodge and Plymouth.

Black Detailing

Among the numerous detailing colors used by Chrysler with the design of these cars, by far, black would have to considered the most used color.

There is something about the black look, perhaps even sinister in some circles. For others it´s a race and performance look. Whatever the reason, there were enough different color uses to satisfy everybody´s mood.

Black Detailing—Hoods

First, let's look at the front end use of black detailing. Sometimes, there were chrome stripes horizontally or a chrome emblem might be centered in the black, but the black always came on strong.

At times, the grille would be split into two equal parts, such as the ´69 Charger, or be completely black like the 1967 through ´69 Road Runners.

With the winged Charger Daytona and Road Runner Superbird models, it was difficult to tell where the grille ended and the hood area began. The triangular front piece smoothly integrated into the hood section. The black color played heavily into the design with the large retractable headlight covers painted dark black.

This ´69 Plymouth Road Runner uses wide black hood stripes to generate a strong racing look.

Black is used to set off the grille area on this ´69 Dodge Charger.

The use of Dodge and Plymouth's black hood detailing is clearly typified on this ´68 Road Runner.

Black striping also was abundant on many of the hoods. The designs varied from a single wide stripe(and sometimes with narrow side stripes along each side), to a pair of two wide stripes (like the ´69 Road Runner), to numbers reversed out of black like the ´71 Duster 340 Wedge or a completely black hood like the ´70 T/A Challenger. With that latter example, the integral hood scoop also was painted black. It looked super mean!

The ´70 Dodge Challenger R/T is all black up front including the hood, scoop, and grille.

Black Detailing-Rear Ends

Just because it was out back, the black detailing wasn´t diminished. The most prominent location for black detailing was the vertical rear valance area directly under the edge of the rear deck. Many times, Mopar performance models also carried a wing on that same rear deck. On models like the ´70 and ´71 ´Cuda, the wing was lifted several inches above the rear deck by two pylons. On the ´70 AAR ´Cuda, the down force device was triangular-shaped and rested directly on the rear deck. The color of each of them was black, of course!

A ´69 Charger R/T aptly demonstrates the use of black on the rear valance.

The rear design of the ´71 Charger included the six taillights and two backup lights housed in a long black strip.

Black was used on the ´70 Plymouth Road Runner Superbird to emphasize its headlight doors.

The twin black rear stripes on this ´68 Charger R/T vividly set off the design.

The rear stripe on this ´69 Charger Daytona actually was a continuation of the black on the tall spoiler wing mounts.

On a ´70 440 ´Cuda, the black is found in the unique wing and the rear valance.

In 1971, one could order a curved stripe on a Charger Super Bee that extended from the hood to the rear of the car.

Some Dodge Challengers carried a full-length body stripe.

Black Detailing—Rear Stripes

There was just something about twin stripes on the rear of their cars the Dodge and Plymouth folks loved. Granted, the stripes could appear in different colors, but be assured, black was the usual choice! With the "winged cars," the rear stripe treatment took on a different look with just a single stripe. It was super-wide and encompassed the huge rear wing. Again, most were black—even though other colors were available.

Black Detailing—Sides

Oh, those glorious sides! There were huge areas for lines and curves (mostly in black) that just blew you away! The most vivid probably was the AAR ´Cuda with its "Morse Code" stripe that curved from front to rear with style and grace. Its termination at the back of the rear quarter was an AAR emblem which stood for Chrysler's "All-American Racing" Trans Am team. Nothing like it has ever emerged since!

The AAR's Trans Am running mate, the Challenger T/A, also was dressed up with a curving stripe that ran from the front of the car to just aft of the door's back edge. Both models also had the black hood.

A number of other models, including the ´71 ´Cuda, also could be ordered with the outlandish (and mostly black) sideboards that completely covered the rear quarters. They reached onto the doors and terminated

The ´71 Charger R/T used an interesting twin black vertical stripe treatment on the forward area of the doors.

In 1972, the Demon used dual black stripes running the length of the body that appeared to increase the width of the rear panel.

with numbers or letters denoting 340, 383, 440, or Hemi. Cars with those additions are very popular with today´s Chrysler muscle collectors.

One of the strangest color combinations with these cars occurred when buyers ordered body and stripes of the same color. Seriously, they did! You can look at a black-on-black combination and it´s extremely hard to even see the stripes! An even stranger look was one Ohio owner who has a pink-on-pink combination!

Black Detailing—Engines

Flat black has always been a signature color for the valve covers of the 426 Hemi engine. Of course, the ignition wires also came out of those valves which

The use of black is seen on the air cleaner cover of this 440-cid engine in a ´70 Challenger.

served in the identification.

Another black appearance in the engine compartment is on the top of some air cleaners. This scheme was available on the ´70 T/A Challenger 440-cid "Six-Pack" engine.

Black Detailing—Wheels

A final mention should be made that black also made its way into that period's wheel designs. It was found in the background of the Magnum 500 wheel, and around the center hub of other wheel designs.

The famous flat black valve covers were standard on the famous 426 Hemi engine.

White Detailing

You don't normally expect to see white detailing, but probably second to black, it was in place in a number of different Mopar applications.

White detailing was used often as demonstrated on this Duster front quarter.

The famous logo and lettering on the AAR 'Cuda really stood out in white.

White Detailing—Names

It was possible to order white name lettering on a number of models. Again, it was done to a level never seen before. The 'Cuda' on the AAR was blocked in white and sometimes the 'Plymouth' was in white on the rear quarter of the Plymouth Superbird. Even the lettering around the cartoon Road Runner on the Superbird headlight covers was done in white.

White Detailing—Stripes

White striping also was available on the rear quarters, many of which contained the model's name. Dodge examples included the ´68 Super Bee and the ´69 Dart GTS.

On the ´71 Charger R/T, it was possible to order a white stripe that traversed two-thirds of the length of the body and terminated on the rear quarters with large letters R and T. And there has been at least one winged-warrior with upper fender reverse scoops that were shot with white paint from a spray gun.

A white detailing variation has been noted on a minimal number of these cars with white side boards,

The use of gray is emphasized in the rear this ´68 Plymouth GTX.

Who could forget Road Runner Superbirds that featured their 'Plymouth' rear quarter scripting in white?

This ´70 GTX is greatly enhanced with unique twin-white-stripes that flow from the hood over the front fenders.

but it is a low number. One thing about the muscle era Mopars, just about anything went, and you could order some pretty strange combinations!

Detailing—Gray

A type of gun-metal gray was used sparingly, but deliciously, in setting up some fine appearances.

Probably the most recognizable use of this color was for the the air cleaner covers of certain Hemi and 440-cid engines. For models with air cleaner covers that came through the hood, it was about as macho as you could get.

That same shade of gray also was used to highlight both front- and rear-end treatments. In particular, the late ´60s Plymouth GTXs used this technique. For the ´68 version, the valance was completely gray with the exception of the red lens inserts. In 1969, the treatment was more intense with even the 'GTX' letters done in the same shade.

For many, the ´70 ´Cuda grille was possibly the best of all the Mopar muscle models. The complete grille was

While it rarely was used, gray appeared on air cleaner covers including this ´70 ´Cuda 440 Six Barrel V-8.

The standard color shade for the Hemi Shaker Hood was this gray tone. It became famous in this application.

Even the Road Runner shows his characteristic yellow bill peeking out from the grille.

This rare rear yellow stripe was an option available on the '70 Challenger R/T.

outlined in gray, including the center bar.

Detailing—Other Colors

Red, yellow, and a rare turquoise were other colors used in interesting ways in these super cars.

For example, red was available but was used sparingly, many times with a white body color that looked very flashy. The color also appeared on the air cleaner cover for certain engines, such as the '68 GTS 340 and '69 Dart Swinger 340-cid engines.

This '68 Dart GTS displays sporty twin vertical red strips that really stand out on this white body.

Yellow was also a portion of the color used in the Coyote Duster air cleaner cover on this '70 Plymouth Road Runner.

Red was used sparingly, but effectively. This 340-cid V-8 in a ´68 Dart stands out in red. Orange normally was used.

The complete block and valve covers were scarlet. The Swinger engine valve covers and block were coated in turquoise.

Yellow also appeared in some very interesting ways, like on the Road Runner´s beak in the grille of certain models, like the ´71 Road Runner.

A yellow dust streak from the Road Runner also has been noted emerging from a body-side scoop and reaching out to the Road Runner himself. The 'Demon' name in the Demon 340 also was done in a bright yellow. The yellow 'Coyote Duster' logo topped the air cleaners of certain engines, like the ´69 Road Runner 383-cid, among others.

Interior Detailing

If you thought the outside and engine bay of these machines had a performance look, you wouldn´t have been disappointed when you opened the doors. It was

Tan was the predominant tone of this ´69 Coronet's interior.

The white interior of the ´66 Charger was dramatic and included a quartet of bold gauge presentations.

The Road Runner character was in plain view, centered in the steering wheel of this '70 Road Runner.

just as sweet, as viewed from the driver's seat.

Although numerous interior colors were available for the Chrysler models, about 95 percent of the buyers selected black. That cold black look just seemed right, no matter what model was chosen. The other predominant selection was the simulated wood grain finish used on the dash, console, and doors.

If you wanted your Dodge interior to be something really special, you ordered the A47 SE (Special Edition) option. Included were bucket seats, sport steering wheel, pedal dress-up, and a wood-grain instrument panel.

Another very available and very-macho addition was the Hurst Shifter, a snazzy performance option to the Mopar interiors. On certain Plymouth Barracuda models, the A62 Rallye Instrument Cluster was available which included a tach, electric clock, 150 mph speedometer, trip odometer with reset, wood grain appliqué, and an oil pressure gauge. The Challenger R/T option included basically the same interior additions.

All in all, interior detailing of this era's muscular Chryslers kept up with the performance and exterior pizzazz—and then some!

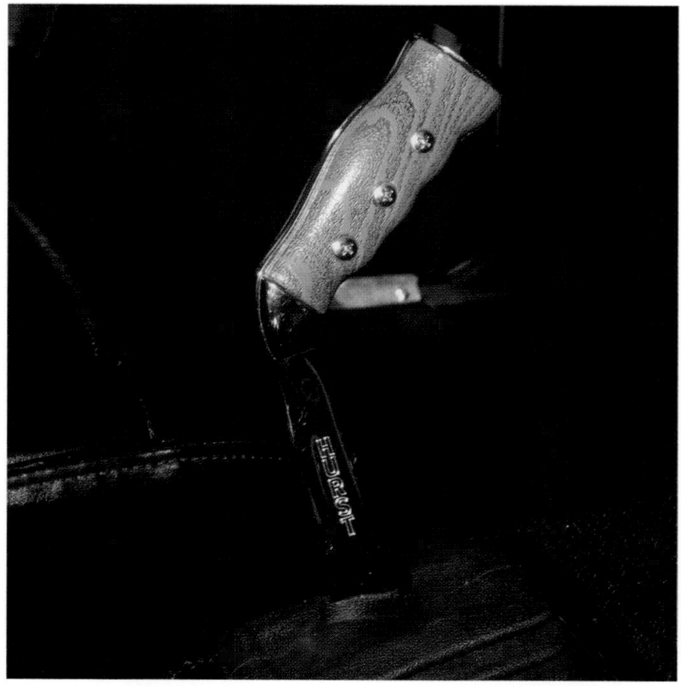

Hurst's Pistol-Grip Shifter was a detailing and performance must for many Mopar muscle machines, like this '74 Road Runner.

Chapter Four: In Your Face and In Your Heart Styling

In addition to all the color, detailing, striping, etc, the Dodge and Plymouth lines also showed considerable styling advances. In fact, the styling meshed beautifully with the "muscle car" aura of the models.

Plymouth styling

Initially, the Barracuda was an outsider to the more glamorous and traditional Chrysler models. It tried to make its own style statement. It began slowly, but by the end of its model run, Plymouth's Barracuda, in many minds, surpassed every carmaker with its ´Cuda option and its completely new style and identity.

Through 1969, the Barracuda remained unique. It had the only split grille design in the complete Chrysler line. During this period, the Barracuda just didn´t carry the macho look of the other models. A new design changed that. First available in 1970, the ´Cuda not only had "the look." It concentrated on the high-performance engines under the hood.

The ´Cuda knocked Plymouth fans out with its body-colored bumpers and rear-quarter stripes. With its smooth, sleek styling, it's not surprising the ´Cuda was picked to be Plymouth Division's entry in SCCA Trans-Am competition.

During the Barracuda's model run, the top-of-the-line model became the AAR ´Cuda. Dolled up in its street version, the AAR ´Cuda looked even better in its race garb.

Along with a decrease in performance in the 1971 model year. Some minor styling changes were made. Four headlights were substituted instead of two, and the newer ´Cudas carried a revised grille. There also were air extractors on the front fenders. The AAR ´Cuda went back to single headlights for 1972.

Plymouth dressed up other models. In 1967, using the basic Belvedere body style, which dated from the early ´60s, Plymouth converted their "Plain Jane" into a luxury performance model. The body took to the upgraded style well and looked good adorned with

The ´71 GTX convertible gives a brutish pose in this view. Note the twin black hood scoops and classic red-striped tires.

Many Mopar fans consider the ´70 ´Cuda the most beautiful of all the classic Chrysler muscle machines.

Note the body-length scallop used on the ´67 Plymouth Belvedere GTX. Later, GTX would supercede the Belvedere name.

optional striping, chrome detailing, and even a pair of nonfunctional hood scoops on the GTX. The long, full-length scallop body styling blended with the new look.

It was possible to acquire a no-frills Belvedere during this time period with the Hemi power plant. There was no fancy striping or detailing, but for those that had the lighter Belvedere body and powerful Hemi combination, that was just fine. They enjoyed surprising the unsuspecting at stoplight confrontations and with this ultimately surprising machine!

For the 1968 model year, the GTX was back with a luxury plus performance image. The styling was cleaner with unencumbered sheet metal on the sides, except for a pair of upper body creases. The GTX was styled with a goal to attract a high-brow audience, but the available 440-cid and Hemi engines still made it appealing to the youth-oriented performance market.

That appeal was enhanced a bit by a pair of twin

The fact this '71 GTX is carrying a 440-cid V-8 is quite evident. The numbers are visible in two places in this view.

A look at the rear of this '71 Plymouth Duster shows the aspects of its sparkling rear design.

The available hood stripe really creates a sporty look on this '70 Road Runner.

The body styling of the '71 Road Runner was a vast departure from previous models. It seemed to possess a more-bulbous look.

The flowing lines of the '71 'Cuda were identical to the '70 model.

low-body racing stripes. Another interesting styling cue was the slight flaring of the front wheel wells. It was a trend that would be continued in future muscle car Plymouths.

A complete change of thinking with the introduction of the 1968 Plymouth Road Runner. Even though the same Belvedere body was used for the GTX and Road Runner, each had a completely different aura. The Road Runner was bare bones and looked like a no-nonsense machine that could be driven directly from the showroom to the local drag strip.

For many, that was exactly what happened. An immediate hit, the Road Runner surpassed sales of its companion Plymouth GTX.

The interior was primitive and the body lacked any ornamentation. That didn´t matter to performance-minded young people who bought it. The only pair of available engines were a hopped-up 383-cid and the 426 Hemi.

Basically, the GTX and Road Runner had the same sheet metal, but again, image and looks went in different directions.

Most people followed the Road Runner's direction

The Plymouth Road Runner was advertised as a stripped-down muscle machine. This ´69 model underlines that impression.

and made it the huge winner in this friendly competition. The production totals of the Road Runner were 82,109 to the GTX's menial 15,010.

That's interesting because of the great similarity of the models, so much so that the options and engine data were usually printed out on the same sheet. The difference, though, was the way Plymouth merchandised the styling and performance of the two versions.

With the Road Runner, it was possible to acquire the so-called "Power Bulge" hood that gave the model the look of a Pro Stock drag racer.

The youth market devoured the Road Runner concept, especially the big engine options. Even in stock trim, with the 440-cid or 426 Hemi engines in place, the styling took on a new look with a forward rake in the body.

Even though the Road Runner was a new car at the time, many owners drove around with that drag-strip, no-wheel-cover-look. It was an image that would hang around for a number of years.

Of the ´69 Road Runner, Tom Shaw of *Muscle Car Review Magazine* wrote in its 1994 edition: "The Road Runner was cocky, confident, and a little crazy. Young guys on the street who lived and breathed performance could relate, even if the corporate pin stripers couldn't... The Road Runner was the Value Meal, no fancy stuff, just lotsa beef to go—hold the side dishes and dessert."

That was the Road Runner, a model that deviated from most of the other Mopar muscle cars of the period, but definitely had a perfect fit with its mostly-youthful groupies.

The styling differences between the GTX and Road Runner narrowed for the 1970 versions. The restyle was identical for both and featured a single rear brake scoop just behind the door.

An interesting image difference occurred with the detailing. The GTX used standard striping. The Road

A popular design, the Plymouth Duster lasted past the 1972 performance engine cut-off and was produced well into the 1970s.

Runner cartoon came into play. It was trailed by a long, narrow whirlwind of dust that followed along from the front fender to the rear scoop.

The styling highlight of the 1970 model year for Plymouth was the Road Runner Superbird. It used a ´70 Road Runner body, then added a conical front nose piece and a towering rear wing. Wind tunnel data helped produce the super-slick look of this low-production model, that's for sure. *(For more data on the Superbird, see Chapters 10 and 11.)*

Even with its futuristic styling, neither Plymouth's Road Runner Superbird nor Dodge's Charger Daytona winged cars moved very well off the showroom floor. A number of sources report the nose piece and wings were removed from Superbirds to convert them back into standard Road Runners.

A little-known fact is the GTX and Road Runner actually were members of the Belvedere family through the 1970 model. After that, the styling guidelines would come from the revised and renamed Satellite series.

Available with Mopar's high performance engines, Dodge's Super Bee looked impressive, especially its bumblebee stripe.

One glance at either the 1971 Plymouth GTX or Road Runner and it was easy to see their styling had changed. The new models seemed to lose some of their macho look and took on a more rounded, bulkier appearance. Some thought they appeared to be more muscular. Others thought they showed a family orientation.

The two models blended during the 1971 model year, each sporting the same non-functional power hood. The design now looked more like the big cars, its front encircled a huge chrome front bumper. The differences in the two models still came in the detailing methods. The Road Runner got over-the-roof strobe stripe, while the GTX was modestly striped.

One of the biggest 1971 design changes was the availability of body-colored front and rear bumpers. They provided a completely different look. And if you had one of that model year's wild colors, it covered just about everything externally.

The ´71 GTX/Road Runner lines brought forth a styling tweak that really gave them a race car look. It was manifested in their extended wheel well flairs. They looked like they could contain a much wider race tire.

Road Runner buyers still clung to a popularly decreasing performance image. They bought their favorite muscle car with a much larger number of Hemi engines installed.

With the decreased emphasis on muscle, the 1972 GTX was eliminated. Plymouth didn't want to completely trash the model. In a strange pairing of two former companion models, it was combined with a Road Runner GTX if the 440-cid power plant was ordered. The model carried the emblems of both models.

The only change to the body styling was a refinement in the rear end. The Road Runner would soldier on for three more model years, but was basically stripped of its performance by changes in the early ´70s. Still, the Road Runner clung to "the look" that had

A rear view of a ´69 Coronet R/T. Although similar to the Charger, the Coronet never got the same publicity or popularity.

served the model so well.

The ´74 Road Runner was particularly striking with its unique, nonfunctional power bulge and a stripe that swept over the rear roofline and forward over the top of the doors, concluding at the outer corner of the headlights.

The Road Runner breathed its final breath in the 1975 model year and by then had lost all the identity of its former styling. The Fury now was the styling base.

For five more years, there was a Road Runner appearance option that could be ordered on the Plymouth Volare. The classic muscle car era was over!

Both Plymouth and Dodge had their compact models, with the former using the Duster nametag. Officially, the model carried the factory name of Plymouth Valiant Duster, but almost everybody referred to it as the Duster, or Duster 340. It was around for four years, 1970 through 1973.

The styling was attention-grabbing with its attractive fast-back roofline and unique tail treatment. With the usual complement of flashy Plymouth color shades, the Duster 340 version really was set off by the black-out hood.

The 340-cid, 275-hp engine was economical muscle. With an 8000 rpm tach and 150-mph speedometer, the Duster 340 met the muscle requirements of many. It still generates considerable interest in the 21st century.

The 1971 sheet metal remained pretty much the same, but the new grille treatment and striping made it look like a new design. Things stayed the same for 1972, but a new front end styling was in place for the final 1973 model. The rear end and grille also showed new characteristics.

Like all the other Plymouth models, the Duster had its kin in the Dodge camp which used the same sheet metal. Dodge followed the 'D' name line by using Demon as its base model name.

Dodge Styling

You have to go back to comparisons. The first Dodge muscle car was the Coronet R/T, which was the Dodge version of the Plymouth GTX, based on the mid-level Coronet body that was similar to Plymouth´s Belvedere. The Dodge Coronet R/T and Plymouth GTX each debuted in 1967, but there was a basic Coronet in 1965 just as Plymouth had its Belvedere Satellite.

There was no mistaking the Coronet R/T for a GTX as the there were considerable differences in the front and rear end treatments. Both used a silver finish consisting of closely attached vertical strips. The taillights actually were illuminated through the material. The non-retractable dual headlights sat in recessed positions on each end of the grille. Centered on the grille was the familiar Chrysler Pentastar. Four

Another "B"-body model, the Dodge Coronet was very popular in its upbeat R/T option version.

nonfunctional louvers sat in the center of the hood to keep the macho look cooking as people joined the "Dodge Rebellion."

A slight change came in the ´68 Coronet R/T with non-functional scoops at rear of the hood along with a hood bulge. Extremely scarce in the 21st century, Chrysler muscle car fans know the Coronet R/Ts had everything the unbelievably popular Road Runners and Chargers had—except the catchy names.

Like the GTX/Road Runner duo at Plymouth, the Dodge Super Bee joined the R/T on the scene. Both were based on the Coronet. Like the Road Runner, the Bee was designed to be basically a no-frills muscle machine.

The innovative ´66 Dodge Charger design was a one-of-a-kind and had the interior volume of a sport utility vehicle.

An attractive split-grille design highlighted the ´71 Dodge Charger Super Bee design.

As both a Chrysler "B" body and a "Bee" car, the Dodge's bumblebee stripes and bee caricature quickly put it out front in popularity, ahead of the slightly older Coronet. The Super Bee's rear stripes contained the circular bumblebee logo and really made the model a favorite.

The mighty Bee was motoring with slicks and wearing a helmet and an awesome pair of goggles. The model fit in well with the Dodge Scat Pack which touted "performance at a new low price."

With its 1968 success, it's not surprising the Dodge Division continued to push the Super Bee in 1969. The sheet metal was unchanged from the previous year, but the taillight panel and grille were modified. The popularity of the Super Bee emblem played a big part. The insect's image now appeared on the deck lid and grille—a stinger that was hard to miss!

The Coronet R/T made the most of its basically unchanged styling. An option that really gave the model a punchy look was a pair of rear quarter scoops just forward of the rear wheel well.

Interestingly, more Hemi power plants were placed in the R/Ts (97) than the Super Bees (92) even though many felt the "Bee" buzzed with more of a performance image.

The 1970 model year would be the last for the Coronet R/T, while the Super Bee would make it through one additional year. Like the rare, one-year-only 1969 Road Runner convertible, the Coronet R/T convertibles also are rare today, even though they were

The coke-bottle design of this '69 Charger was recognized as revolutionary for its time period.

The '68 Charger was one of Mopar's largest sellers during this era. Its styling makes its popularity easy to understand.

produced over several model years. Dodge's new "B" body styling was carried through in both the Coronet R/T and Super Bee models. Each wore a distinctive front bumper design. The R/T looked tough with a single protruding scoop on each rear quarter and a revised six-light rear panel. The hood also showed a pair of recessed, nonfunctional scoops.

An easy way to define the ´70 Super Bee was its pair of hood scoops. The R/T's cool rear side scoops weren't included on the Super Bee. The Bee logo also appeared in the front center of the hood. Interestingly, the final 1971 Super Bee would switch from the Coronet to the Charger platform.

Mention Dodge performance during this era and most likely, you'll hear people recall the Charger. Undoubtedly, that great name caught everybody's attention and it had the looks and performance to match anyone's automotive fantasies.

The Dodge Challenger was very similar to the Plymouth ´Cuda.

The Demon was an upstyle version of the Dart in the early 1970s. This 1972 model has stylish twin hood scoops.

The Dodge Charger first appeared in the 1966 model year. Where other Chrysler Corporation models shared sheet metal across company lines, the new Charger was unique and original. Quite frankly, the Charger looked more like a limousine than a leopard. Wide and sleek, its fenders stood tall throughout the length its body. The body-length scallop covered a majority of the side area. And it sported its trademark fastback.

The Charger's interior was totally unique. All seats reclined and created a wagon or camper usefulness. The Charger didn't begin with the performance/ muscle car image, though you could get a Hemi with it. The Charger evolved into possibly the top Chrysler-made muscle car.

The styling of the ´67 Charger was pretty much the same as the previous year, but everything changed in 1968. What evolved in the new Charger was a performer that now carried the R/T designation. The styling was more curved and presented a big-time racing image. It was the first design to be tabbed by publications of the period as having the "Coke-bottle" image.

The sheet metal remained status quo for 1969 with changes occurring in the grille design. It got a center divider and new taillight treatment. Two additions to the 1969 Charger line were the Charger 500 and Charger Daytona.

The great Charger look remained in place for the third straight year in 1970, but added a chrome loop bumper and a backward-facing R/T scoop that was placed just in front of each door. While it was totally nonfunctional, the scoops were a great styling touch.

The Dodge Charger has to rate as one of the unique Chrysler muscle cars of this special era, not to mention one of the top cars of the late ´60s and early ´70s.

The 1971 model year meant muscle car producers began facing a number of problems—such as increasing insurance for their performance models. Some companies bowed and did away with their powerful muscle models. Dodge thought their Scat Pack Group machines still had some life left in them. The super-popular Charger kept up the styling, even though the power was down.

With the Coronet version of the Super Bee gone, one of the Chargers took on the Super Bee identity. It paid homage to the "Bee," but the revered Charger swoop still was in place. The Super Bee included the decals on the hood and side panels, yet this bee buzzed with confusion. It was very similar to Plymouth retaining the GTX as a Road Runner option.

The ´71 Charger´s styling was altered with a new fastback roofline and split-grille redesign. Ventless side windows and concealed windshield wipers added to the new Charger looks.

Then there was the Challenger, Dodge's response to the Plymouth ´Cuda. The 1970 Challenger's main motivation was to qualify for Trans Am racing.

With a two-inch longer wheelbase than the Barracuda, the Challenger was a styling extravaganza that featured a "hang-over" front end, four headlights and a recessed grille. Body sides were similar to other Dodge models of the era with the expected coke bottle

The Challenger was Dodge's "E"-body counterpart to the ´Cuda. Detailing gave this ´70 Challenger its own look.

look and kicked-up rear fender.

The T/A version looked like a racer and so did the top-line Challenger R/T version. Its curving, race-style stripe followed the body contours, optional rear spoiler, blackout grille and rear end. You couldn't go wrong. Fitted with the available Hemi mill, it was an ultimate example of the Scat Pack and "Dodge Fever" generation in motion.

In 1971, during the second of its five years, the Challenger received a few styling changes with the R/T getting a split grille, fake brake scoops in front of the rear wheel cut-outs, and wider body stripes.

It was back to the drawing board for the 1972 Challenger with completely-new front end styling. Some thought the new look moved away from a performance image. For example, the R/T no longer was the power version. That honor belonged to the Challenger Rallye.

Challenger styling featured strobe stripes emerging from a simulated scoop just behind the front wheel well. A restyled rear-end and widely-spaced fake hood scoops also were in place.

As the Challenger moved toward extinction with its ´73 and ´74 models, the changes were minimal. It still had a great power look, even though its under-the-hood performance was fading away.

Like Plymouth, Dodge had the "D" family of compact versions. Dodge's camp played heavily on its Scat Pack Performance Group publicity. Dodge had its GTS and Demon 340 options for two years, in addition to the Dart.

The Dart line first saw the light of day in 1965, but didn't draw attention until 1968 when the model took on the Scat Pack persona. The ´68 and ´69 styling was pretty much the squared-off design of the original. The colors, striping, black-outs, and emblems put them with the Scat Pack's big boys. Although the big engines weren't available (except with special factory race versions) you could still special-order the 383-cid mill.

The ´68 GTS was a huge hit with the performance clan. It was fully decked out with rear bumblebee stripes, Rallye Wheels, black-out grille and rear end. Its performance-appearance hood made this a "killer bee." Reportedly it was even possible to acquire a 440-cid big block!

The Demon name appeared in 1971, officially called the Dodge Dart Demon 340. The Demon was a direct response to Plymouth's Duster 340. Each had identical body shells with different front and rear treatments. Basically, styling remained static for the final "muscle year," 1972.

Even though the punch under the hood had departed, similarly-detailed Darts continued under the Dart 340 Sport, followed by Dart 360 Sport model which featured an added larger-displacement engine.

From this tough stance, you know this '69 GTS is one tough performance machine.

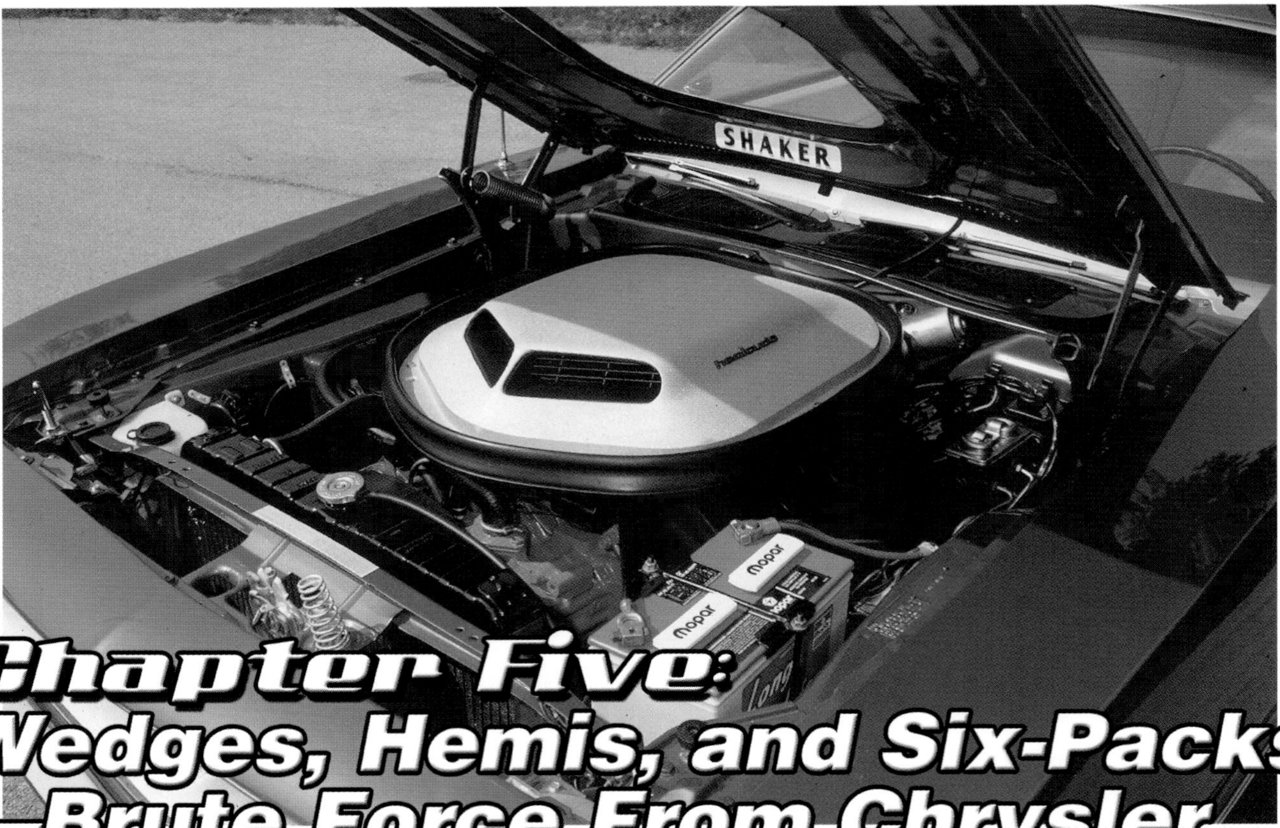

Chapter Five: Wedges, Hemis, and Six-Packs —Brute Force From Chrysler

Those engines! Those magnificent Chrysler power plants that provided the abundant horses! For many, they were the highlight of all the Chrysler muscle car models.

Like the cars themselves, the engines seemed to have a life of their own. They definitely were important in the overall mood of the models. Their presence and identification were displayed prominently on the sheet metal in many different ways and in highly-visible locations.

For many owners of Chrysler products, the engine that rested under the hood was the most important aspect of their personal machine. Having a 426 Hemi or a 440-cid Six-Pack engine bolted into the engine compartment, and the fact that it was announced externally, told of the power under the hood. It was a real ego-builder just to be behind the wheel of one of these machines!

The Hemi of its time was an awesome machine, but in about 1964, Chrysler considered building a dual overhead cam (DOHC) Hemi version for race applications. Changes in NASCAR rules caused its cancellation.

The famous Hemi name still is very much alive. The new Hemi made its first appearance as part of the 300C

Everyone knew the Hemi's 426 cid. This emblem was mounted on a number of Hemi-powered machines, including this '68 Super Bee.

This golf club or hockey stick-shaped rear quarter stripe was a popular addition for this '70 Cuda with a Hemi engine.

The Six-Pack 440 is revealed on this ´70 ´Cuda with the "´Cuda-440-6" identification.

Chrysler concept car in 2000. The new engine will be considerably smaller than the original 426-cid. With just 5.7 liters, it shows a considerable 345 hp.

Announcing the Engines

There never was anything like it considering the engine size—and sometimes the induction technique—that was broadcast on the body. With the muscular performance models during this period, there never was any doubt what was putting the "oomph" to the rear wheels.

Depending on the model and year, the ultimate Hemi "Elephant" engine was presented in several different and highly visible ways. For example, on the ´68 Dodge Super Bee, the Hemi name was printed in black on a brushed aluminum plaquel. On the ´70 ´Cuda, the name appeared in large letters on the rear quarter at the termination of a body stripe.

The ´71 Road Runner showed the name in letters that appeared along with the Road Runner cartoon.

If you really wanted the world to know your engine's cid, you ordered a sideboard stripe, as is shown on this ´71 383 ´Cuda.

While most of the Chrysler engines were known by their displacement numbers, Chrysler simply spelled out the "Hemi" name, rather than using the "426" displacement numbers. "Hemi," or the displacement numbers for the other engines, also appeared with the popular wide sideboard stripe in the 1970s.

The 440-cid engine, available with single four-barrel or three two-barrel carburetors, also received significant attention on the cars' exteriors.

The importance of the engine type was demonstrated on the ´70 ´Cuda where the 440-cid engine was combined with the model name. For example, "´Cuda 440-6." The "6" indicated the six barrels of carburetion.

On the ´70 Charger R/T, the six-barrel carburetion

This ´70 Charger R/T has its Six-Pack induction system identified on both sides of its functional hood scoop.

was proudly proclaimed on the hood scoop as "Six Pack." On that same model, the sheet metal was adorned with "440 Six Pack," featuring the two words in red. The technique was the same for the Challenger R/T and its 440 Magnum power plant.

On the ´70 Road Runner, the black-out hood had "440+6" on either side with the "+6" in orange. You never knew what the Chrysler folks would design. The aforementioned sideboard also was available on the ´71 ´Cuda, among others. The "440" numerals appeared mid-body on each side. As the performance of the era spiraled downward in the early 1970s, so did the pizzazz of engine identification. The ´72 GTX had the 440 numbers in a black decal below the chrome GTX model designation.

The 383-cid and 340-cid engine designations were similar to that of the 440-cid, but the Trans Am racing version(the Challenger T/A) carried the nomenclature "340 Six Pak" in large numbers and letters on the front quarter.

Preceding the Hemi in popularity was the Max Wedge like this one found in a 1964 Dodge Coronet. (Angelo Van Bogart/ OCW)

The Hemi nickname was used on versions of the powerful mill, including the catchy "Hemi Head" from this ´70 Charger.

This ´70 Duster advertised its 340 Wedge for all to see with this nomenclature angled on the hood.

Probably no other model provided engine identification like the ´70 Challenger T/A, which carried it on the front quarters.

The 383-cid numbers for the ´67 Plymouth Belvedere were carried in the hood ornament.

The "440 Six Barrel engine" compartment of a ′70 Plymouth Road Runner is shown here.

Hemi orange was the dominant 440 engine color on a ′69 Dodge Daytona. The air cleaner carried the "Magnum" name.

The Hemi engine for the ´66 Charger and others showed a chrome air cleaner cover and the flat black valve covers.

The ´70 Superbird and other Chryslers used a rectangular-shaped orange air cleaner cover with black "Hemi" lettering.

This Ramcharger device provides a closed-air connection between the hood and engine on this ´70 Superbird.

Dodge called the three-carb induction set-up a "Six Pack" as shown here.

The ´71 Dodge Super Bee and other ´71 Dodge 383 models topped their air cleaners with chrome.

The Engine Compartments

As stated earlier in the book, the engine compartment sheet metal carried the same color as the external sheet metal. Through the years, one predominant color was used in the engine itself.

Not surprisingly, Hemi Orange was used on a vast majority of the blocks and was used on valve covers, air cleaner covers, and other engine-associated items.

The ´71 383 cid Road Runner's air cleaner carried the "383 Road Runner Engine" complete with the famed cartoon icon on top.

Notice the little-used bright red on the block, valve covers and air cleaner top of this ´68 Dodge Dart GTS.

"340 Four Barrel" was the lettering on top of the air cleaner of the ´70 Dart Swinger, among Chrysler-built products.

Also, there were engine-peculiar color detailing practices. In Dodge applications, the 426 Hemi engine used a chrome air cleaner cover and the ever-distinctive flat-black valve covers. It was a color that continues to be used on modern versions of the infamous power plant.

The ´69 race-oriented Challenger T/A carried the 340 Six Pack air cleaner style.

Plymouth didn't want to appear to copy its Dodge competitor, so it used a 440-style air cleaner cover for its Hemi versions. The "Hemi" name was lettered in black.

With the 440-cid engine, the differences under the hood continued between the divisions. The 1969 Dodge Charger Daytona's round air cleaner cover featured an orange top with "440 Magnum" lettered in black within a circle.

The 1970 Plymouth Road Runner, with a 440-cid engine complete with a six-barrel carburetor, used an open rectangular air cleaner done in orange with a "Coyote Duster" decal.

When the 1970 Plymouth Road Runner Superbird used the six-barrel 440-cid V-8, the Ramcharger induction hood attachment was done in the Hemi Orange. The ´70 440-cid four-barrel version carried the

The ´70 AAR ´Cuda's engine compartment was identical to the Challenger T/A with the exception of the "Six Barrel" name.

A pair of functional hood scoops grace the hood of this ´69 Dodge Super Bee Hemi.

"Aggressive" would describe the functional hood scoop style on this ´67 Dodge Coronet with its 426 Hemi engine.

"Super Commando" designation, lettered on the top cover of the air cleaner.

As the muscle era came to a close, earlier rules that had governed the engine compartment began to be followed loosely.

For example, the ´72 Plymouth GTX had its block, intake, and valve covers done in a bright blue.

The same rules basically were followed with the 383-cid engine. One interesting deviation was the lettering atop the 383 Road Runner combination. The

One of the wildest functioning hoods was the Air Grabber which was retractable and functional and looked exciting.

The hood layout for the E71 Challenger and its 440 Six Pack has a clean design and was efficient in operation.

The 440 engine's hood treatment definitely was ornamental, but clearly displayed the ´72 Satellite's engine displacement.

The twin scoop arrangement on this ´71 Duster 340 was macho and extremely effective.

white lettering announced "383 Road Runner Engine."

There were a number of 340-cid engine appearance variations during the period. A completely-different look was in place for the ´68 Dart GTS. The block, intake manifold and valve covers all were done in a bright red. With the four-barrel carb in place, the black lettering on the red air cleaner's top said "340 Four Barrel."

The Trans Am models—Plymouth's AAR ´Cuda and the Dodge Challenger T/A—used the same 340-cid engines with triple-carb set-ups. Everything was identical—with the exception of the decal on the air cleaner top.

The AAR was labeled "340 Six Barrel" with white lettering on a white background. The T/A did it a little differently with "340 Six Pack" done in red-and-white lettering with a black background.

The "Pack" was spelled without a "C" on the car's exterior, probably to match the "Six."

Dodge produced an attention-getting ad about the punchy 340 engine headlined "6,000 rpm for less than $3,000."

Hood Treatments

During the muscle car era, both Dodge and Plymouth devised designs that advertised and augmented the power just below the hood.

A large and functional Pro-Stock-style hood scoop was available for the Hemi- and 440-powered Coronets, Super Bees and other Dodge models. The distinctive appendage straddled a major portion of the hood area.

In 1967, a macho-looking hood design showed its face sporting a pair of functional scoops. These air-gatherers, available on a number of models, started at the rear of the hood and terminated midway. They definitely looked mean!

The scoops were available for a number of different models at various times during the muscle car period including the Plymouth GTX and Dodge Coronet R/T, Demon, Dart, and Super Bee. It also was possible to order the performance engines in conjunction with the dual scoops.

Most Chrysler muscle car fans will point to the "Shaker Hood" style that fed the 1970 and ´71 Hemi engines. With a menacing glare, the bulbous device looked like a UFO emerging from it's landing site.

Usually gray in color, it gave a ´Cuda or other models a "rompin'-stompin'" appearance. Thats what many remember most about these cars. Lift the hood and the "Shaker" name was in blurred letters like the engine was running. But it wasn´t!

The AAR ´Cuda hood was entirely different from the Challenger T/A with its single, centered, functional scoop.

But they didn't stay around long and were replaced with blander, nonfunctional hoods. The ´71 Road Runner, for example, had a rectangular protrusion on the hood that did exactly nothing.

On certain ´69-´70 models, such as the Road Runner, the dashing and functional "Air Grabber" hood was available with the 440-cid and Hemi-powered machines.

There really was nothing like it. A lid closed flush with the hood surface. When it was functioning, the "Grabber" lid raised about 30 degrees, revealing a cartoon character on each exposed triangular side. Reportedly, it wasn't a good idea to open the "Grabber" when it was raining!

The Mopar engine compartments in these muscle models were as wild as the outsides of these cars!

A view of the Pro Stock-style hood scoops on a trio of ´70 Challenger T/As, which use the 340 cid engines.

This ´70 340 ´Cuda's hood sports a pair of neatly-recessed hood scoops.

Chapter Six: Grabbers, Road Runners, and Bees—Magic Mopar Names

The use of unique names. The internal and external locations of those names. Names used in the engine compartment. The Chrysler muscle cars offered something never tried before in the American automotive industry.

There's an ever-present speedy bird peering out from the grille of a '71 Road Runner.

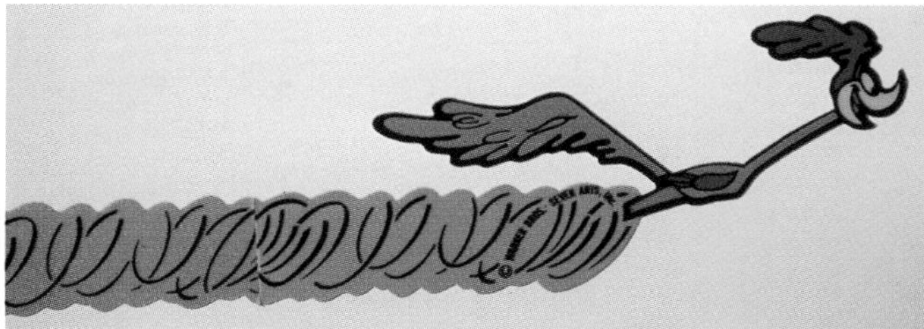

Many times, the Road Runner was shown in motion as this '70 Road Runner with a gold trail of dust following his blazing feet.

The names they used sometimes represented living things (like the bee in Super Bee) and or the sport fish, the Barracuda. There were popular cartoon characters used for models such as the Warner Brothers Road Runner, licensed by Chrysler, or the Coyote Duster, with Wile E. Coyote. In addition, Chrysler's Air Grabber, Demon, and Duster all had unique cartoon characters.

Also, there were a number of names that exuded performance and a macho impression including Challenger, Charger, Dart, Fury, and others.

The famous bird character appears within the rear deck stripe on this '70 Road Runner.

The Road Runner also was present after the performance era, resting here in rooftop stripe of a '74 Plymouth Satellite.

Here, the Road Runner logo is a part of a "Morse code" stripe of this '71 Road Runner.

In addition, there were multiple-letter identifiers that pointed toward racing—like GTX, R/T, T/A, GT, GTS, and others.

During those golden muscle car years, Dodge and Plymouth did everything to make those names as visible as possible, placing them strategically on all parts of the models. Some ended up in the most unexpected places.

The Road Runner

Certainly the most famous of these names was the infamous and speedy desert bird Road Runner cartoon character. He was a long time favorite, famed for his classic chases with Wile E. Coyote. And the way he was

The Road Runner logo often was contained in a circle as he's shown here on the rear deck of a '72 Road Runner.

To view the location of this Road Runner, you have to raise the hood and find the unique "beep-beep" horn on this '70 model.

Slide behind the wheel of a Road Runner and the bird greets you from the horn button. He's just about everywhere you look.

This air cleaner depicts Wile E. Coyote viewing a cloud of dust left by the Road Runner on this '70 edition.

The warp-speed Road Runner was honored on this headlight cover. He was "promoted" on this Plymouth Superbird.

displayed on that Plymouth model made him a legend.

Only once did the always-losing Coyote appear on a Plymouth machine. That occurred on certain engine air cleaner covers.

The speedy little Road Runner was everywhere on

The Road Runner cartoon even appeared on the gas cap of this '72 Road Runner GTX.

the model of the same name! The model continued into the 1970s, even though the performance it represented had long since departed. He was definitely the star of the line.

Much of the time, the Road Runner was represented in motion, with swirls of dust cascading out behind him. In some cases, that dust reached back along the

side of the car's body.

And on the ´71 Road Runner, his three-dimensional head poked out of the black-out grille. He wasn't that big, but the effect really got your attention.

The "Air Grabber" hood revealed a creature with razor-like teeth and open mouth gulping air to feed the engine below.

Here the Duster is embedded in a white stripe above the displacement figure on a ´72 Duster 340.

One of the biggest uses of the Road Runner was in body stripes. The ´70 Road Runner had a horizontal stripe across the bottom of its rear deck. On the right side of the stripe, he stood looking very coy.

On the ´71 model, there was an available dotted stripe which reached completely over the roofline. He resided in the base line square on each side, moving at full speed.

On several of the ´70s Road Runners, he was encased in a circle. The words "Plymouth Road Runner" flowed around him in the circle.

The speedy bird also was part of one of the most unique and memorable aspects of the car. The car's unique horn replicated the "beep, beep" of the Road Runner. The horn was colored in a light violet with the Road Runner's smiling face and the words "Voice of Road Runner." Press the horn and you heard that distinctive sound. Pretty cool, for sure!

Slide behind the seat of many Road Runners and there he was peering upward from the steering wheel hub. The smiling face is there along with the words: "Beep! Beep!"

This special Duster Twister has the character swirling from a black racing stripe on this ´72 model.

The Duster was a highly-visible cartoon. All you could see was a pair of eyes peering out of the swirling dust cloud.

He even appeared on some air cleaner covers, such as the ´69 383 model. He was in the outer ring along with the words, "383 Road Runner Engine." And on certain models, the yellow-beaked bird was even on the fuel cap and on the dash. Busy little guy. Literally, he was everywhere!

The largest versions of the Road Runner appeared on the low-production, high-performance Superbird instead of the standard models. Even though it was still the Road Runner caricature, the company decided to give the Road Runner a promotion—to Superbird.

Encased by those words, the symbol of Plymouth's most awesome model carried the logo on each side of the tall-standing wing struts. And he was in place on the left side blackout headlight door.

Reportedly, Plymouth's marketing department didn't immediately appreciate the addition of a cartoon on their beautiful muscle machine.

Through the 1968 model year, the Road Runner cartoons appeared in black and white. But the frenzy created by the bird brought him into full color for the remaining years.

In retrospect, the cartoon made a lot of sense since the Road Runner was designed for speed and performance. A stripped-down body and the big horsepower engines definitely made it a "Road Runner." The car was capable of sub-15 second performances in the quarter mile. The Road Runner was everywhere!

A bee powered by a pair of racing slicks inspired Dodge's Super Bee name. This one appeared on the tail of a ´69 Super Bee.

Air Grabber

It's hard to describe the cartoon character that Plymouth called the "Air Grabber." He (or it) was visible only when the hood scoop system was functioning and providing cool air to the carburetors.

The cartoon character appeared on the sides of the scoop as though it was drinking in air. When it was closed, the words "Air Grabber" sometimes were printed on each side of the scoop's top.

Raise the hood, and there it was again on the underside of the hood flange. The flange enabled a solid connection between the hood and top of the engine.

Duster

That crazy little "Duster" cartoon. What was it? The Duster character is hard to define. All you could see was a pair of eyes peering from a whirlwind of dust clouds.

A real eye-catching logo, it appeared mostly on the rear quarters and rear valances of the 1970s Dusters. For example, the ´70 Duster 340 model

How's this for dedication? This Super Bee owner has the little bee tatooed on his arm.

The ambitious little bee got its face on the hoods of some Super Bees, this one a ´71 model.

The mischievous Demon endowed certain 1970s Dodge Darts. His three-pronged fork doubled as the "M" in the Demon name.

featured the caricature superimposed between the rear parallel stripes. The Duster 340 lettering was directly to the right of the Duster cartoon—which was done in gold, black, and white.

In 1972, the Duster logo was contained within a body stripe. For black stripes, the Duster was done in white—and vice versa for white stripes. On the Duster "Twister" version, the dust whirlwind was about twice as long, emphasizing the twister.

Super Bee

The mischievous little insect, the "Super Bee," sported a racing helmet and it rode on a pair of racing slicks.

The most familiar location for this awesome insect was a part of the car's rear end detailing. The ´69 Dodge Super Bee and other models carried a vertical bumblebee striping display that carried a circular Super Bee logo. The bee was centered in the circle with the Super Bee lettering surrounding it.

Certain Super Bee models also mounted the bee on the rear valance. Another highly visible location for the bee was on the special vented hoods that featured the 1971 383 Magnum and other engines. The logo stood out against the blackout portion of the hood.

Although it never appeared on any of the muscle cars of this era, the Dodge "Scat Pack" name also used a bee character in its advertising. The "Scat Pack" bee resembled the Super Bee. He was also complete with helmet and burning-rubber racing slicks.

Demon

A Dodge cartoon created some mild controversy.

The R/T name on this ´67 Coronet R/T convertible got the attention of performance-minded buyers. It was done in red.

Reportedly, certain religious groups objected to the "Demon." Looking like a little red devil, he carried a three-bladed fork which created the "M" in the Demon name. It appeared on the ´71 Demon, in association with the 340-cid engine it carried. The "340" appeared in a number of different locations, including in front of, in back of, and below the lettering.

R/T

Although not a cartoon character, "R/T" was associated with many models. An option package—models such as the Challenger, Charger, and Coronet—all benefited from the performance aspects of those famous letters.

Depending on the model and year, the R/T logo appeared in both a chrome emblem and in decal form. With the ´70 Challenger R/T, the identification was a part of the body-side stripe, directly under the Challenger name, which was above the stripe on the front quarter panel.

On the ´71 Charger R/T, the logo was carried in body color on the black portion of the hood. The ´68 Charger R/T carried the R/T lettering in chrome in the front grille and mid-body just in front of the door crease.

The´70 Challenger R/T logo was contained in the body-length stripe directly under the Challenger name.

The R/T on this ´70 Challenger R/T is actually larger than the nameplate, emphasizing the importance of the performance option.

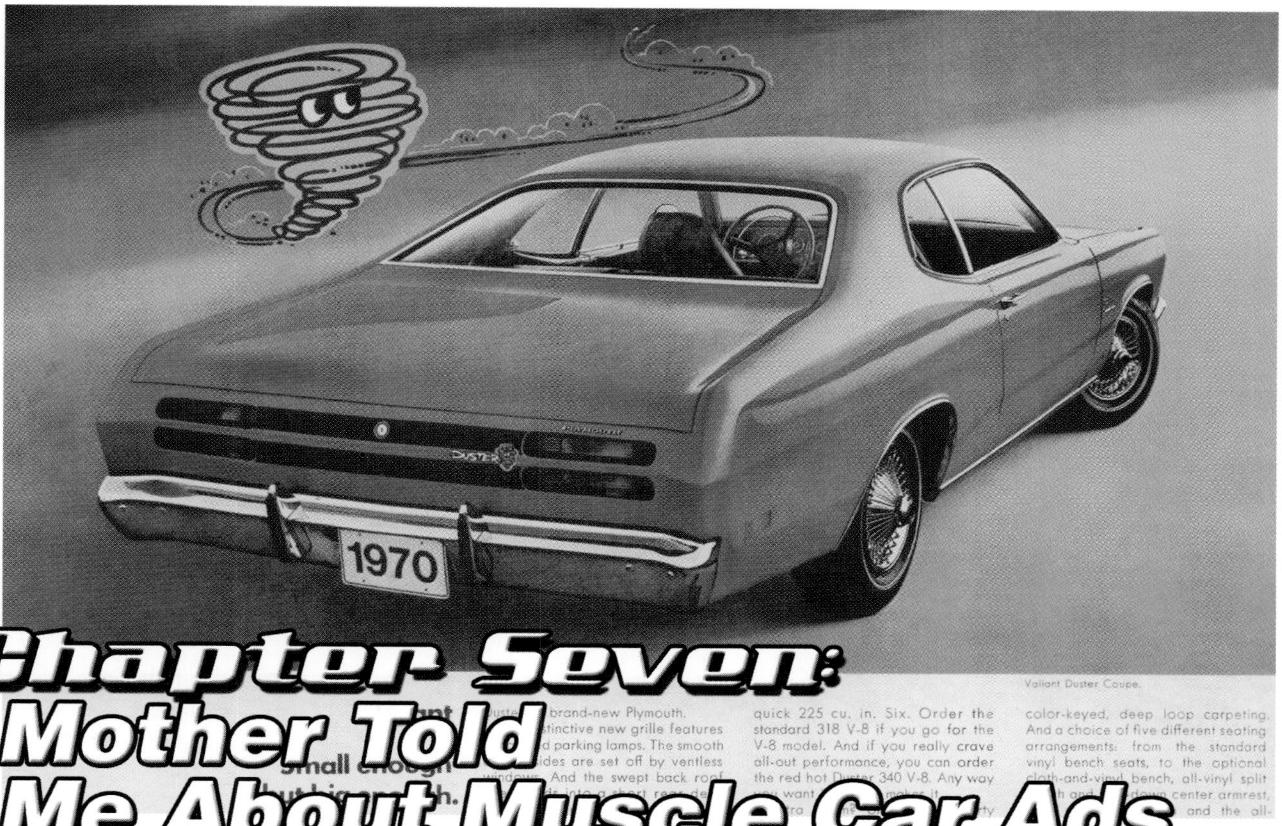

Chapter Seven: Mother Told Me About Muscle Car Ads

The Chrysler car scene was crazy in the muscle car era, and the out-of-sight advertising that passed on the virtues of the models was equally wild and crazy.

In order to stay up in the Big-Three-plus-AMC auto manufacturing race, Chrysler marketing had to load all the artillery. It was a big-time war. Every major manufacturer, and most of the divisions, had muscle machines they were doing their darndest to move off the showroom floors.

Plymouth and Dodge were heavy players and innovative contenders in this performance confrontation. The advertisements that were produced by the two Chrysler Divisions took highly divergent directions. Each of the Mopar lines were uniquely outrageous!

Plymouth used garish drawings and cartoons to emphasize the burning power of its models. Dodge went about the task in an entirely different manner with its striking models. They said the right things and used majestic photos.

Plymouth Advertising

Initially, the Plymouth muscle car advertising style was pretty calm. All that changed in 1967 with the work of artist Dale Dalton whose main focus was the car's dimension distortion. Certain aspects of the models were widened and foreshortened, giving the cars a highly-aggressive look. His main concentration was on the Road Runner.

In 1968, the cartoon characters became a part of Plymouth's national advertising, including the Road Runner and Wile E. Coyote. (Plymouth advertisement)

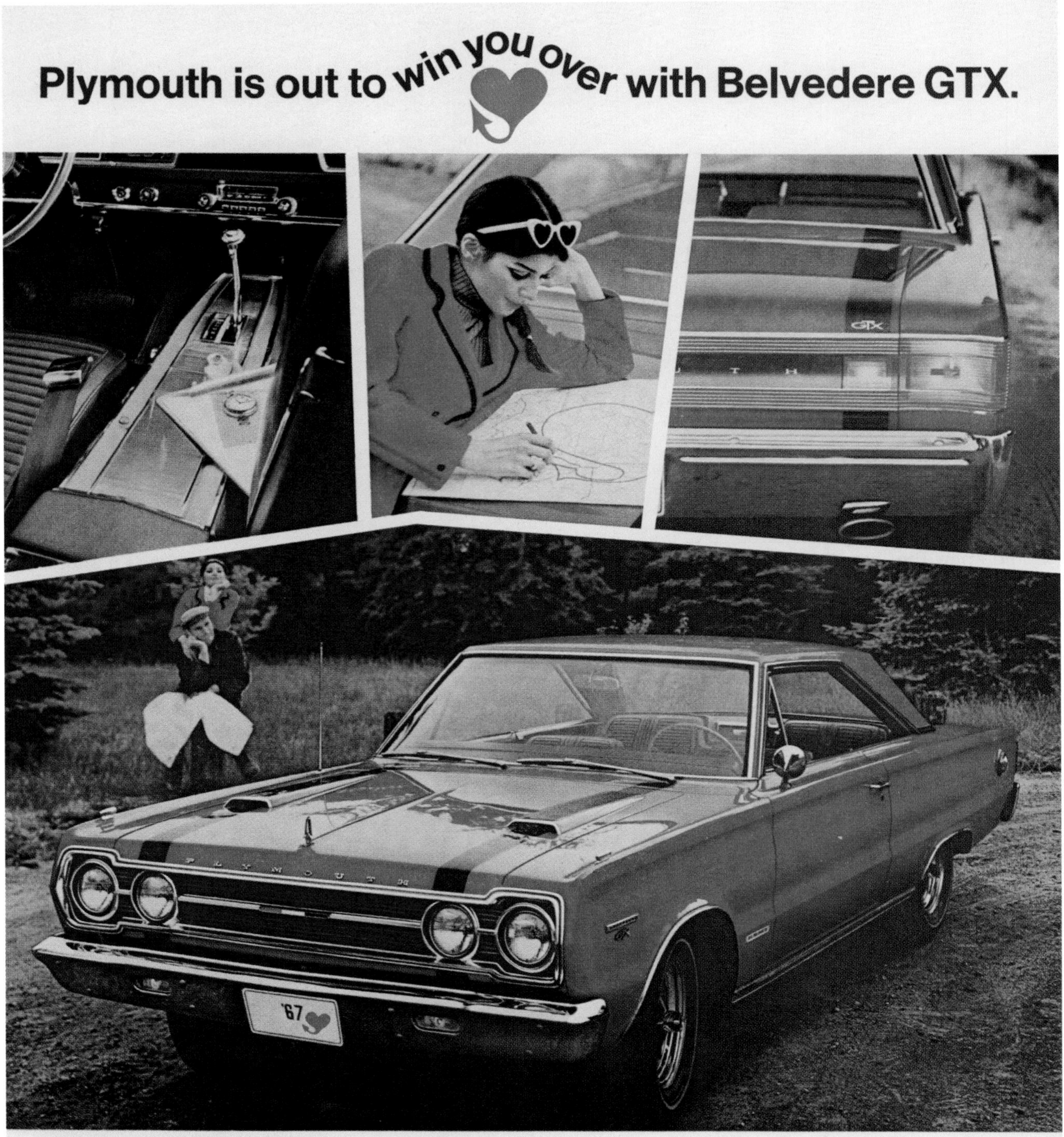

Plymouth is out to win you over with Belvedere GTX.

GTX. Plymouth's exciting new Supercar. King of the Belvederes. Standard equipment: the biggest GT engine in the world. Our Super Commando 440 V-8. Optional equipment: the famous Plymouth Hemi.

This Plymouth goes flat out to win you over. And there's nothing hidden about its promise. Check the twin hood scoops up front, twin chrome exhaust megaphones out back.

Note how the GTX sits up on its special suspension. Obviously, this is something special—right down to the new pit-stop gas filler, Red Streak tires, chrome valve covers and custom, no-nonsense grille.

Now, if this Belvedere is a little heady for you, we've got 21 other models—all with varying degrees of devilment—out to win you over.

Be prepared to be persuaded.

Plymouth

This ´67 Plymouth GTX ad advertised the performance of the Super Commando 440 V-8 engine. (Plymouth advertisement)

Tires were fattened with billowing clouds of smoke rolling off them in great gobs. Model names were greatly enlarged, and the words that went with them were 'hip,' to say the least.

The cars had a distorted look—and even sported drag racing-type open exhaust headers projecting from their undersides. Those headers resulted from a little freedom taken by the illustrator. No such equipment was available with those models. If the fantastic cartoon power was in place, the illustrator decided it was necessary to "get those ponies to the pavement." The cartoon Plymouths were equipped with drag racing tires. And the tires carried low inflation with ripples on the sidewalls.

One of the classic pieces of Dalton magic appeared in the June 1968 *Hot Rod Magazine*. It was a head-on shot of a distorted, fire-belching Barracuda.

The car is on a drag strip. You are looking head-on at its out-of-proportion lines. The starter tree is in the right background. The ad carries only a one-word caption: "Shortcut."

The accompanying ad copy has nothing but words about the super performance available from its awesome power train. The ad is directed to a customer who would know the "hows and whys" of engines and transmissions.

It reads:

"The heads are new and have big 2.3 inch ports. The intake valves are 2.08 inches in diameter and the exhausts are 1.74. The cam provides a .425 inch lift on intake and .437 on exhaust ..." You get the idea.

Can you imagine such racing tech wording in a modern car advertisement?

The ad also offered a factory contingency award to any Plymouth that took a Stock Eliminator title at an NHRA National or Regional event. The ad concluded with: "The Plymouth win-you-over beat goes on."

In the 1969 model year, Plymouth took its advertising technique to new and totally-outlandish levels. Artist Paul Williams was the new main man and the direction definitely was aimed at the youth market.

Williams took the Dalton caricatures one step further with his wild-and-crazy 1969 Hemi Road Runner Car of the Year ad. The Road Runner was depicted coming off the line in a drag mode. The front end was up, rear drag slicks digging in, and hot exhaust gases cascading from an exhaust pipe just behind the right front wheel. If that wasn't enough, the headlights appeared to be gazing skyward.

In another Williams creation, there's a shot of the

Engine: Standard is a 440 cu. in. V-8, with high-lift cam, Carter AVS 4-barrel, 2.08 in. intake valves, 3.2 sq. in. ports, cast-iron headers and stiffer valve springs. Compression is 10.1 to 1; horsepower is 375 at 4600 rpm; torque is 480 lbs-ft. at 3200 rpm. Optional is Chrysler's famed 426 cu. in. Hemi, which uses things like a nitride hardened crankshaft, two Carter AFB's, solid lifters, forged aluminum pistons and tulip-shaped intake and exhaust valves. Compression on the Hemi is 10.25 to 1; horsepower is 425 at 5000 rpm; torque is 490 lbs-ft. at 4000 rpm.

Transmission: Standard on all 440 cu. in. GTXs is a manually-shiftable, competition-type TorqueFlite automatic with an 11¾ in. diameter torque converter. Special features include five front clutch discs instead of the usual four, a 2½ in. wide second gear band, an oil cooler and internal oil filter. Hemi-powered GTXs carry a similar unit, but with a 10¾ in. diameter converter. Optional to both is a heavy-duty 4-speed with coarse-pitch gears and ratios of 2.65, 1.93, 1.39 and 1.00.

Rear axle: Heavy-duty on all GTXs. Automatic-equipped cars carry an 8.75 in. diameter ring gear, while 4-speeds use a 9.75 in. unit. Final drive options range from 3.23 to 1 up to 3.54 to 1.

Suspension: Heavy-duty everything: including front torsion bars, ball-joints, stabilizer bar and front and rear shock absorbers. The rear springs are stiffer than normal, too, and the right spring carries one more leaf than the left, to prevent torque steer under acceleration. Spring material is chrome steel with plastic innerliners.

Tires: F70X14 Wide Profile.

Brakes: Standard front drums measure 11 x 3 in.; rear drums measure 11 x 2½ in. Total swept area is 380.1 sq. in. Front disc brakes are optional.

As you can see, GTX is something of a departure in automobiles. A rapid departure. Hence, we recommend that it be driven very carefully on the street, and the full use of its potential restricted to organized drag events.

At the strip, however, it's a different story: when the light turns green, we urge you to politely bid competition "Adio-o-o-o-o-s-s-s!"

...the Plymouth win-you-over beat goes on.

Write for four 24 in. x 17 in. full-color cartoon posters of GTX, Road Runner and Barracuda. Send $1.00 to: Posters, Dept. C, P.O. Box 7749, Detroit, Mich. 48211.

GTX. That's short for "Adios!"

440

GTX

Plymouth

CHRYSLER MOTORS CORPORATION

Ads for the 1967 Plymouth models started to have a bloated look with belching headers, and smoking tires. (Plymouth advertisement)

Everybody offers a car. Only Plymouth offers a system.

Heck, anybody can build cars with big engines. Plymouth's Rapid Transit System is a lot more than that.

As the name implies, it's a system; a total concept in transportation that goes far beyond eight pistons and a steering wheel.

The Rapid Transit System is racing—at Daytona, Riverside, Cecil County—and the race cars themselves—Dragsters, Super Stocks, Oval Stockers—the essence of high-performance machinery.

The Rapid Transit System is information—the straight scoop from Plymouth to you—tips on how to tune your car, modify it, which equipment to use, and how to set the whole thing up for racing. For a free brochure on all that's available, just write *Rapid Transit System—Dept. A, P.O. Box 7749, Detroit, Mich. 48231.*

The System is person-to-person contact—us and you—at Supercar Clinics conducted throughout the country by our own racers.

The System is high-performance parts—now conveniently packaged and available through your Plymouth dealer.

Above all, the R.T.S. is the product—everything from a Valiant Duster 340, all the way to a Hemi-'Cuda with a quivering Air Grabber. Each car in the System is a *complete* high-performance car, with suspension, brakes, driveline and tires to match.

Compare Plymouth's Rapid Transit System with mere cars.

And if you can't beat it—join it.

grille and "Six-Pack" hood of a Hemi Road Runner. The air cleaner tops of the carburetors can been seen looking through the hood scoop. Again, the illustration gives the impression of the cars being alive.

As quickly as it started, all the wild-and-crazy cartoons suddenly were shelved forever. An unbelievable era had quickly come and gone. Nothing like it had ever been seen before and probably nothing will be in the future.

It got a lot milder for the 1970 season with actual photographs of Chrysler muscle models coming back

The success of Plymouth's Superbird in NASCAR competition wasn't overlooked in the division's period advertising. (Plymouth advertisement)

Plymouth emphasized the racing aspects of the Superbird, showing it as a stripped car with a number of features deleted. (Plymouth advertisement)

Acceleratii rapidus maximus. That's Latin for the fact Plymouth's Road Runner is some other kind of bird. Hang in here a moment, and we'll show you why.

Body: Road Runner's traditionally a 2-door coupe with a hardtop look. But now, by popular demand, there's also a real, live hardtop version available. Both configurations, however, feature welded unit-body construction, which means they won't rattle like cement mixers after the miles pile up. Furthermore, you can now order the coupe Bird with a new decor package—including a premium all-vinyl interior in your choice of eight colors.

Engines: the standard Road Runner powerplant is an exclusive version of our 383 cu. in. V-8. Heads are borrowed from the big 440 cu. in. GTX engine because of massive intake and exhaust valves, 3.2 sq. in. ports and stiffer valve springs. The cam, intake manifold, valve train and exhaust headers are likewise GTX in origin. Resultant compression is 10.1 to 1; horsepower is 335 at 5200 rpm; torque is 425 lbs-ft. at 3400 rpm. Optional on all Road Runners is our 426 Street Hemi, which produces 425 hp at 5000 rpm and 490 lbs-ft. of torque at 4000 rpm.

Transmissions: standard on all Road Runners is a fully synchronized 4-speed. A manually shiftable, 3-speed TorqueFlite automatic is optional.

Rear axle: standard ring gear diameter on all 383 and Hemi automatic Road Runners is 8.75 in. 4-speed Hemis carry a 9.75 in unit. Final drive ratio on all 383s is 3.23 standard, 3.55 optional. Hemi automatics also carry a 3.23 ratio as standard, with our 3.54 Sure-Grip differential available as an option. Hemi 4-speeds carry the 3.54 gear, standard.

Suspension: heavy-duty torsion bars, shock absorbers, rear springs, ball-joints, front stabilizer bar. Hemi-powered Birds use extra-heavy-duty rear springs with six leaves on the left, seven leaves on the right, for directional stability under acceleration.

Brakes: all Road Runners carry big 11x3 in. drums in front, 11x2½ in. drums in back. Front discs are optional.

Tires: F70 x 14 Wide Tread.

Horn: "Beep-Beep!"-type unit.

But before you take off on any coyote hunts, remember one thing. Hunt only at organized drag events.

Do that and Plymouth might even pay you money. Win Stock or Super Stock Eliminator at a NHRA National, and Plymouth will pay you $400.00; win Stock Eliminator at a Regional, and Plymouth pays $250.00. That way, coyote hunting's not only safer—it's downright profitable.

...the Plymouth win-you-over beat goes on.

Write for four 24 in. x 17 in. full-color cartoon posters of GTX, Road Runner and Barracuda. Send $1.00 to: Posters, Dept. C, P.O. Box 7749, Detroit, Mich. 48211.

Road Runner.
(acceleratii rapidus maximus)

Plymouth

CHRYSLER

This radical national ad shows a '68 Road Runner with headers smoking and racing slicks throwing a whirlwind of fire. (Plymouth advertisement)

into vogue. There also was an emphasis on the 'Rapid Transit Authority' nomenclature to identify the stable of Plymouth muscle cars.

One of the most amazing advertisements of that era was a two-page spread that showed all the RTA cars across the top, with an amazing table filled with performance data below on each model. From cartoon caricatures to technical data—what a change in direction!

The Charger R/T SE, a beautiful model and sexually charged double entendre copy—a reflection of late ´60s America! (Dodge advertisement)

Period Dodge Advertising

Dodge diverted from the norm in advertising during this period, but it was far from the direction and wildness of the Plymouth Division.

Where the Plymouth boys used the "Rapid Transit System" for its fleet of muscle-bound "go-machines," Dodge used the two-word nickname "Scat Pack" for its "A"- and "B"-body bombers. And where Plymouth had used its Road Runner logo to typify the "Rapid Transit System," a feisty version of the Super Bee character stood for Dodge's "Scat Pack."

The bee sported a pair of slicks and a helmeted head with racing goggles. It looked like it was tooling along at 100 mph just sitting still. Scat Pack ads often used a head-on version of the Bee.

The basic Super Bee logo also identified the Dodge model in its logo which was used prominently in the rear bumblebee stripes.

The Scat Pack, along with the RTS, both were involved with Supercar Clinics that traveled around the country and featured big-name racers. The Scat Pack Club also rewarded its members with a number of performance-associated goodies.

Special catalogs emphasized factory performance parts, club jackets and decals, and even factory tune-up folders.

It should be noted that Dodge always emphasized road safety through its Scat Pack ads with statements such as: "Drive safely, it's contagious," and "Don't be caught dead wrong-drive safely."

During the muscle car era, certain Dodge ads that didn't carry the Scat Pack theme still were pretty sprightly with shots of the cars at obviously high speeds. The ads even included some burn-out shots.

A proud Road Runner stands by its Plymouth namesake. Everything about the car seemed colorful and bigger than life. (Plymouth advertisement)

It speaks softly, but carries a big kick. Dodge Coronet R/T. Just about the hottest thing going since the cast-iron stove. Witness these credentials: a rampaging 440-cubic-inch Magnum V8 that deals out 375 bhp and 480 lbs.-ft. of torque. 4-barrel carb . . . long duration cam . . . chrome engine dress-up . . . low-restriction dual exhaust . . . heavy-duty brakes and suspension . . . high-performance Red Streak tires . . . special air scoop design. With this standard getup, R/T is described by Super Stock magazine as "one of the best all-around performance packages being offered . . . as much or more performance per dollar than any other car currently available." If you wish, you can have the optional Hemi. And a tach. And mag-type wheel covers. And a lower-body paint stripe available through your Dealer. Check out R/T at your nearby Dodge Dealer's now.

This '67 Dodge Coronet R/T ad emphasizes its performance aspects. It quoted a compliment from* Super Stock *magazine. (Dodge advertisement)

RUMBLE BEE

Want to start something?
Try a hot-cammed 383-cube mill in a light coupe body.
Just for kicks, throw in the heavy-duty suspension,
oversized brakes, a brute of a hood, bumblebee stripes
—the works. It's tough. Check the price. Good news!
Dodge has started something all right. Super Bee.
Why sit there dreaming when you could be running? See
the man with the cars with the bumblebee stripes.
Your Dodge Dealer.

STANDARD SUPER BEE EQUIPMENT

● Special 4-bbl. 383-cid V8 (has the 440 Magnum V8 heads, valve gear, hot cam, and manifolds), 335 hp at 5200 rpm ● Dual exhausts ● 4-on-the-floor manual with HD clutch ● HD suspension ● HD shocks ● HD brakes ● Dodge Charger Rallye instrument panel ● F70 x 14 Wide-Treads.

OPTIONAL

The Hemi-425 hp.

Dodge Scat Pack ... the cars with the Bumblebee stripes

DRIVE SAFELY—
SPEED CONTESTS BELONG ON THE STRIP

Dodge CHRYSLER MOTORS CORPORATION

"Rumble Bee" emphasizes the performance orientation of both the Dodge Super Bee car and the "Dodge Scat Pack" identity. (Dodge advertisement)

This 1970 Challenger R/T ad plays on words about the car's Plum Crazy color. This Dodge "Super Grape" gets our attention! (Dodge advertisement)

Performance was fading in 1971 but the same couldn't be said for Dodge's attention to the Demon 340 and Charger Super Bee. (Dodge advertisement)

Dodge

CHRYSLER
MOTORS CORPORATION

Announcing:
CORONET "SUPER BEE"
Scat Pack performance at a new low price.

Run with the Dodge Scat Pack

Beware the hot cammed, four-barreled 383 mill in the light coupe body. Beware the muscled hood, the snick of close coupled four-speed, the surefootedness of Red Lines, Rallye-rated springs and shocks, sway bar and competent eleven-inch drums. Beware the Super Bee. Proof you can't tell a runner by the size of his bankroll.

These specifications are published for the uncommon interest:

POWERPLANT: Standard: 383 CID V8. Carb: 4-bbl. Compression ratio: 10:1. Special camshaft: Lift (Intake, .450; Exhaust, .465). Duration (Intake, 268°; Exhaust, 284°). Overlap: 46°. Valves, hydraulic (Intake, 2.08 head dia.; Exhaust, 1.74). Intake manifold: Equal length four branch low-restriction type. Exhaust: Dual. Horsepower: 335 at 5200 RPM. Torque: 425 lbs.-ft. at 3400 RPM. 10.2 pounds per horsepower. (Dry.) Air cleaner, unsilenced, both standard and optional V8.

Optional: Hemi 426 CID V8. Hemispherical combustion chambers. Carb: dual, 4-bbl. Compression ratio: 10.25:1. Camshaft lift (Intake, .490; Exhaust, .480). Duration (Intake, 284°; Exhaust, 284°). Valves (Intake, 2.25 head dia.; Exhaust, 1.94). Intake manifold: Cast aluminum dual level with heat shield. Exhaust manifold: Special cast-iron low-restriction exhaust headers. Horsepower: 425 at 5000 RPM. Torque: 490 lbs.-ft. at 4000 RPM.

TRANSMISSION: Standard: Four-speed full synchromesh manual. Ring block synchromesh. Floor-mounted shift. Gear ratios with std. eng.: 1st, 2.66; 2nd, 1.91; 3rd, 1.39; 4th, 1.00.

Optional: TorqueFlite Automatic three-speed. Column-mounted shift. Gear ratios: 1st, 2.45; 2nd, 1.45; 3rd, 1.00.

SUSPENSION: Heavy-duty springs and shocks, all four wheels. .94-inch dia. sway bar standard.

BRAKES: Heavy-duty standard on all four wheels. 11-inch drums, cast iron. Shoes: 11"x3", front; 11"x2½", rear. Lining area: 234.1 sq. in. Front discs optional. Self-adjusting Bendix type. Swept area, 387.8 sq. in.

ADDITIONAL OPTIONS: High-performance axle package consisting of 3.55 axle ratio with Sure Grip. High-capacity radiator, 7-blade slip-drive fan with shroud.

INSTRUMENTATION AND APPOINTMENTS: Padded Rallye-type dash standard, matte black, includes circular speedometer, oil and temperature gauges, electric clock. Matching tach optional. Matte black grille, power hood, Red Line wide-tread tires, seat belts, front shoulder belts, carpeting, foam seats, bumblebee striping and special ornamentation standard. Vinyl roof optional.

RACING JACKET OFFER Show your stripes right away. Order your special all-nylon, red Scat Pack racing jacket. Comes in sizes for everyone! Men: S-M-L-XL-XXL. Women: S-M-L. Children: 6-8-10-12-14-16. **Send $9.95 for each jacket (check or M.O.) to Hughes-Hatcher-Suffrin, Shelby at State, Detroit, Michigan 48226.**

SPECIAL OFFER Write: Dodge Scat Pack HQ, Dept. F, PO Box 604, Detroit, Michigan 48221. **Send me the Scat Pack decals, lapel badges and catalog of goodies. Here's my quarter.**

Name____________________

Address____________________

City__________ State________ Zip______

Car Owned: Make________ Model________ Year______

The cartoon bee represents the Dodge Scat Pack moving at high speeds and introducing the 1968 Coronet-based Super Bee. (Dodge advertisement)

The Super Bee conveyed motion. The Bee rode racing tires and wore a helmet and goggles. The bee's body, antennae, and wings were swept back to show all-out motion.

This Road Runner wears Plymouth's "Win Your Heart" logo on his racing helmet and has a big smile. "Beep Beep Baby" is a lighthearted takeoff on his favorite line.

1973 Dodge Charger Rallye. For the hard driving man.

If you're the kind of man that responds to the pulsating beat of a performance car, grab hold of Charger Rallye. Charger's got the low, lean look that tells you exactly what it is—a performance machine that enjoys being on the road. Go ahead, get in. Settle your frame into Charger's optional, soft bucket seats. Turn the switch on this beautiful baby. Charger's new Electronic Ignition System will give you surer starting because it delivers up to 35 percent more voltage to each spark plug. Then pop the clutch on Charger Rallye. That optional floor-mounted, four-speed Hurst shifter and 440 four barrel will let you put this Rallye through its paces. Charger's rugged Torsion-Quiet Ride and front and rear sway bars can take it. This go anywhere, do anything Charger Rallye can be an expression of whatever you want it to say. And those no-nonsense Rallye instrument gauges say a lot about the car and the man who uses them. When you take off with that power bulge hood and those raised white letter tires, there's one thing sure, you'll be remembered . . . as the hard driving man.

Extra care in engineering makes a difference in Dodge...depend on it.

Dodge's 1973 Charger Rallye portrays a rugged car and notes features like a Hurst shifter, the four bbl 440 engine, and more for the "... hard driving man." (Dodge ad)

Wanted: Men who can handle a real road machine. Dodge Challenger Rallye.

There are special men who develop an almost spiritual attachment to their cars. They want a no-nonsense road machine that grabs a rough, winding stretch of road and holds on. One that stays low and close to the road like a snake. For these men, Dodge builds Challenger Rallye. A trim, taut, tough car that hugs every inch of road it goes over. Why? Because of Challenger's torsion bar suspension. No mushy coil springs for this car—only responsive torsion bars and leaf springs will do. They combine to give you a firm, honest ride all the time.

These special men will also appreciate Challenger's Electronic Ignition System. Because there are no points and condenser, this system is virtually maintenance free and your tuneup costs will be reduced. Neither wet nor weather affect this special system. And each spark plug will get up to 35 percent more starting voltage every time.

Dodge Challenger Rallye. A special kind of road machine for a special breed of men. Test-drive one at your nearby Dodge Dealer's today.

Extra care in engineering makes a difference in Dodge...depend on it.

The Dodge Challenger Rallye from 1973 also targets young males, but appeals to handling characteristics. It proclaims to be "... for a special breed of men." (Dodge ad)

DAYTONA INDIANAPOLIS PHOENIX RIVERSIDE LANGHORNE ATLANTA CHARLOTTE POMONA HARLINGEN AUGUSTA BRIDGEHAMPTON ASCOT YORK HARRISBURG DARLINGTON CONCORD COVINGTON VINELAND DETROIT DALLAS MEMPHIS BRISTOL

Where will you see Chrysler Corporation's new hemispherical engine in action?

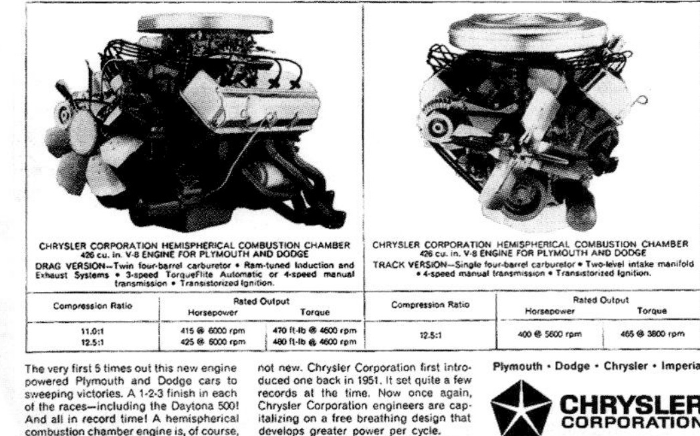

CHRYSLER CORPORATION HEMISPHERICAL COMBUSTION CHAMBER
426 cu. in. V-8 ENGINE FOR PLYMOUTH AND DODGE

DRAG VERSION—Twin four-barrel carburetor • Ram-tuned Induction and Exhaust Systems • 3-speed TorqueFlite Automatic or 4-speed manual transmission • Transistorized Ignition.

Compression Ratio	Rated Output	
	Horsepower	Torque
11.0:1	415 @ 6000 rpm	470 ft-lb @ 4600 rpm
12.5:1	425 @ 6000 rpm	480 ft-lb @ 4600 rpm

CHRYSLER CORPORATION HEMISPHERICAL COMBUSTION CHAMBER
426 cu. in. V-8 ENGINE FOR PLYMOUTH AND DODGE

TRACK VERSION—Single four-barrel carburetor • Two-level intake manifold • 4-speed manual transmission • Transistorized Ignition.

Compression Ratio	Rated Output	
	Horsepower	Torque
12.5:1	400 @ 5600 rpm	465 @ 3800 rpm

The very first 5 times out this new engine powered Plymouth and Dodge cars to sweeping victories. A 1-2-3 finish in each of the races—including the Daytona 500! And all in record time! A hemispherical combustion chamber engine is, of course, not new. Chrysler Corporation first introduced one back in 1951. It set quite a few records at the time. Now once again, Chrysler Corporation engineers are capitalizing on a free breathing design that develops greater power per cycle.

Plymouth • Dodge • Chrysler • Imperial

CHRYSLER CORPORATION

Two Hemi engines with specs. One is for drag and the second for track racing. The heading includes some of America's most famous racing sites. Simple and powerful. (Chrysler Corporation ad)

They don't call it King Kong for nothing.

Not hardly. A car doesn't get a name like that on looks alone. Not when it walks off with Top Stock Eliminator at the '66 Springnationals, Winternationals, Summernationals and World Championship Finals. Not when it idles like this one does. Not when it turns 11-second ETs and makes the trip sounding like—well—just ask the guy up there holding his ears.

This, you see, is a Hemi-powered Belvedere. More specifically, a Belvedere GTX. The Hemi part costs extra, and the car itself is specially set up for drag racing. But impressive? Man, it's devastating!

Your next question should be: *Do we build a street version of the GTX? With maybe just a little less hair?*

Glad you asked. We do indeed, and it comes with our 440 cu. in. (375 hp.) wedge-head as standard equipment. It also comes with a special heavy-duty suspension, hood scoops, Red Streak tires, wide rims, bigger brakes, low-restriction exhausts and a heavy-duty TorqueFlite automatic—again, it's all standard.

And if you order it with the 4-speed, you get coarse-pitch "Hemi" gears, a heavy-duty rear axle, viscous-drive fan, unsilenced air cleaner and a dual-point distributor as part of the bargain. Sound King-Kongish, too? It is. Because Plymouth is out to win you over. **'67 Belvedere GTX**

Plymouth

CHRYSLER
MOTORS CORPORATION

A 1966 Plymouth Belvedere GTX is portrayed as a noisy drag machine, complete with irritated adult. King Kong appealed to kids who wanted an outrageous dragster-like car. (Plymouth ad)

A unique ad for the 1968 Plymouth GTX is written like a song and repeats the Plymouth tag line "And the beat goes on" like a chorus. Cars and music mixed well in this era. (Plymouth Ad)

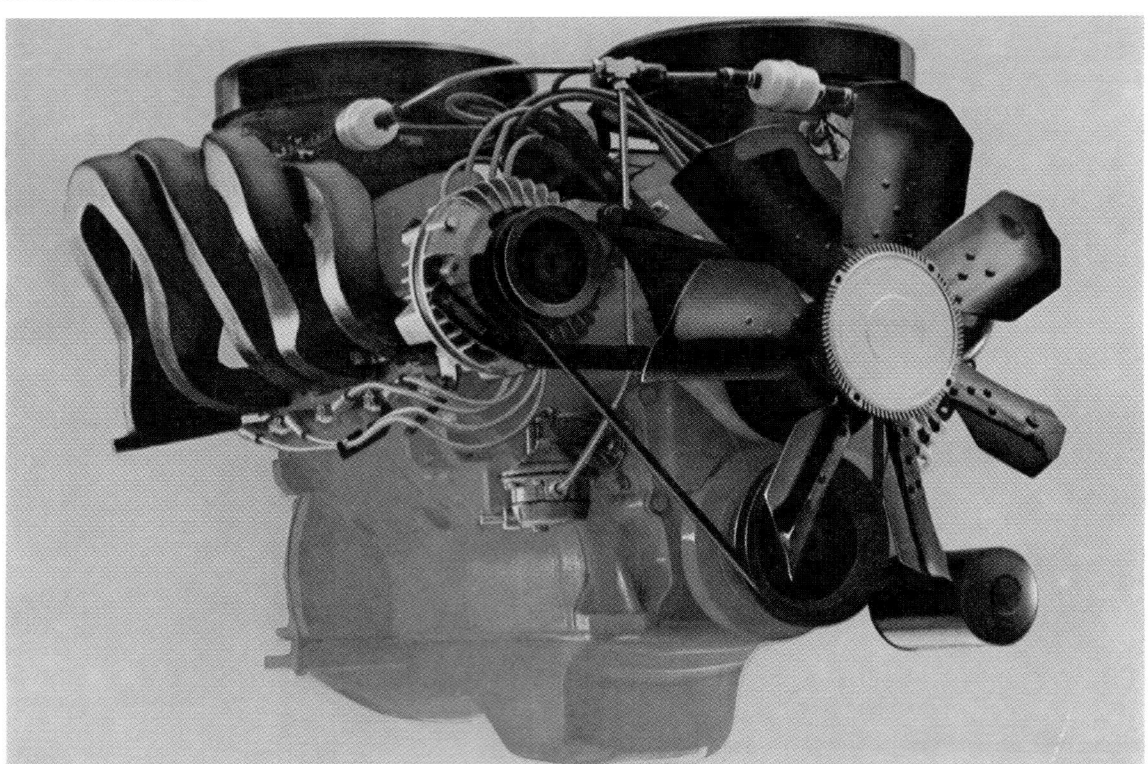

The Dodge Ramcharger/Plymouth Super Stock 426, was as "in your face" as muscular engines got in 1964. This angle plays up the iron manifolds with Tri Y headers. (Chrysler Corporation ad)

The quickest.
(Duster 340)

And the newest.
(Duster Twister)

Aha! Could it be Plymouth has now come through with not one, but *two* Duster Supercars?

Well, not really.

It's just that we've come to the conclusion that the most appropriate way to show off our newest Duster (the Twister) is to show it sitting next to our quickest Duster (the 340).

To look at it, you'd never know that beneath Twister's sleek fastback shell lies one of our 198, 225 or 318 cubic inch engines. The ones that are looked upon with favor by insurance companies, are easy to take care of and don't drink much gas.

Every Twister comes with the unique Duster 340 grille.

It has bias-belted tires and 5½" Rallye wheels without trim rings.

And we've added racing mirrors, flat black hood performance paint, strobe stripes, side stripes, lower deck stripes and optional hood scoops.

Combine all this with torsion-bar suspension (for good handling), solid unibody construction, room for five and an incredibly low price . . . and what more could you want?

The Duster 340, maybe?

The Rapid Transit System. Coming through.

Plymouth

CHRYSLER

Plymouth's Dusters were all muscle. Rallye wheels, hood scoops, stripes, flat black sections, special grilles, and more meant two "Duster Supercars" to choose from. (Plymouth Ad)

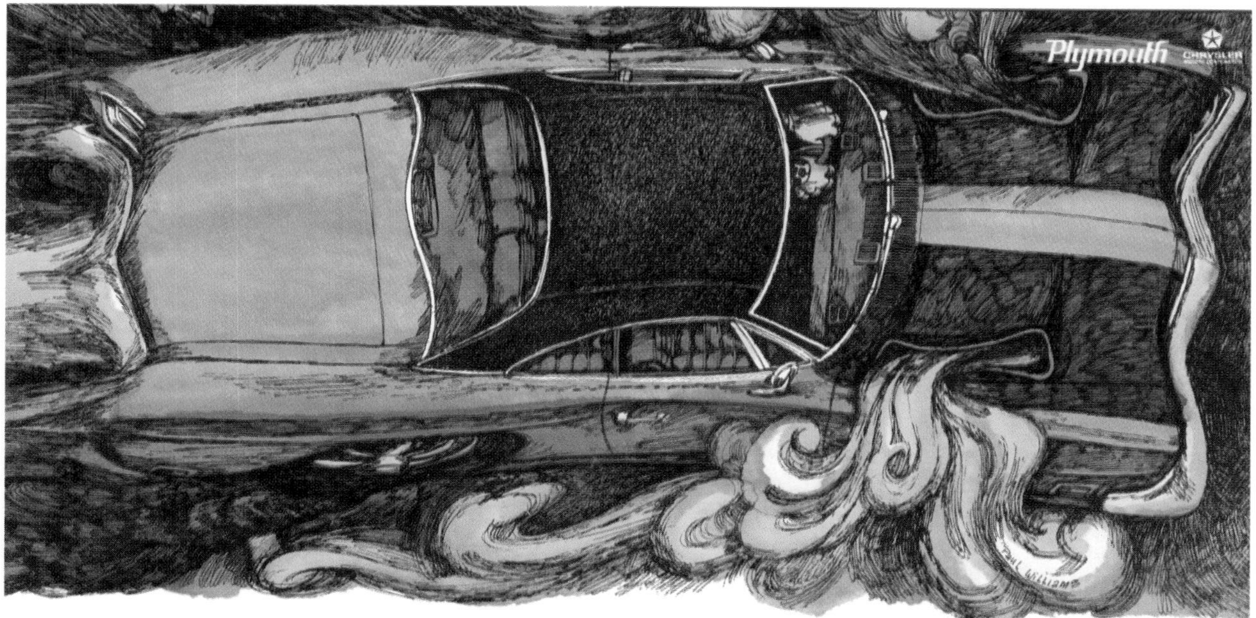

BEEP-BEEP! EEEYYOWWWW!

PLYMOUTH TELLS IT LIKE IT IS.

See test results, page 123

CUDA 340 STORMS THE QUARTER RIGHT IN FRONT OF NHRA AND EVERYBODY

PLYMOUTH TELLS IT LIKE IT IS.

For a copy of Plymouth's wild new high-performance car catalog, send 50¢ to Supercars, P.O. Box 7749, Dept. R, Detroit, Michigan 48207.

Mod and psychedelic art styles were evident in these late 1960s Plymouth ads with highly stylized, full color caricatures of the cars.

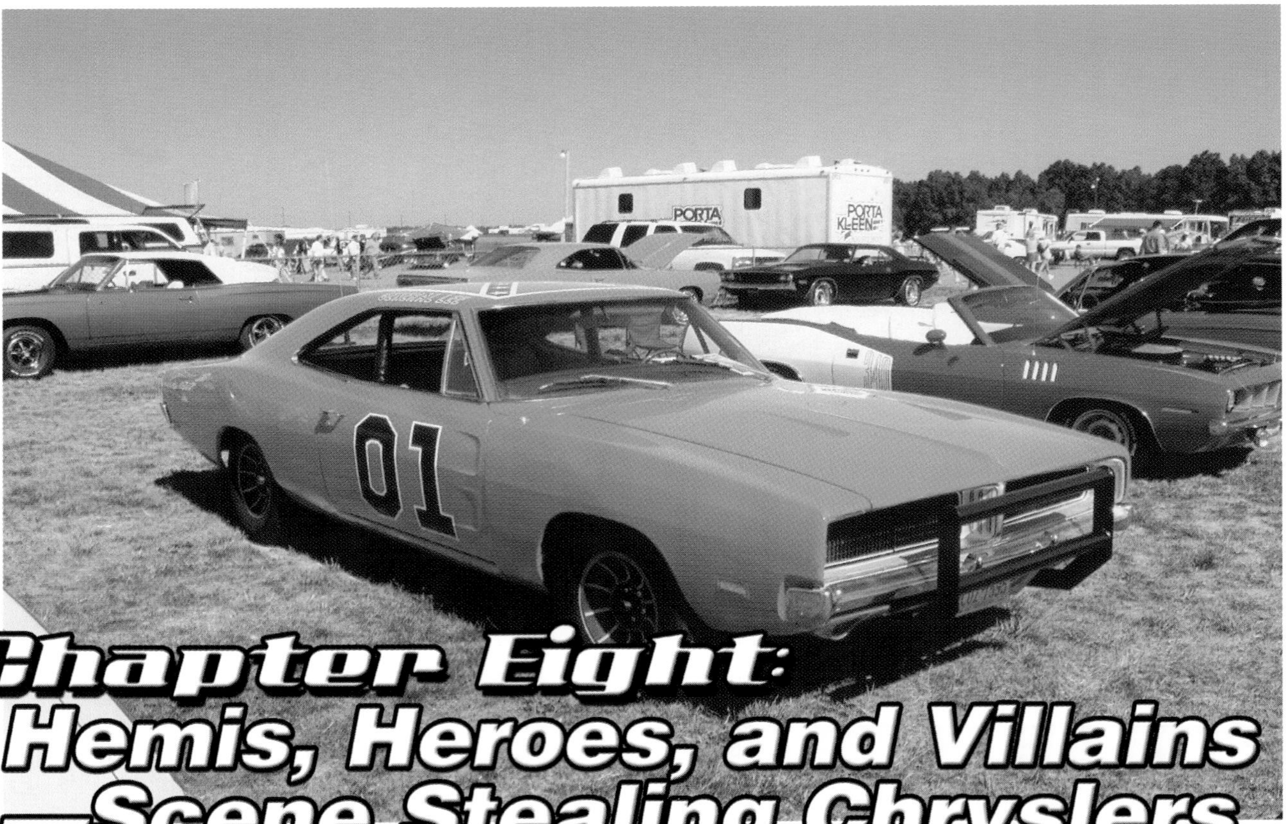

Chapter Eight: Hemis, Heroes, and Villains —Scene Stealing Chryslers

A major percentage of the Chrysler exposure of the 1960s and 1970s came from the actual vehicles on the street and their exposure through national advertising and racing.

There were two other unlikely sources for exposure. One was through their amazing appearances (mostly with Chargers) in movies and TV series. Another was their use as state and local police vehicles. Mopars were

A black ´68 Charger R/T, like this one except for small wheel covers, co-starred in the classic Bullitt *with Steve McQueen. (Dodge-Charger.com photo)*

on the scene and in the scenes!

There are a number of examples of each of these sources. You'll be amazed at how these models were used.

Movies

Bullitt

One of the most memorable movies of 1968 starred Steve McQueen, along with a ´68 Charger. *Bullitt* was the movie. To this day it is recognized as having one of the best chase sequences ever! Unfortunately, the Charger ended up in a ball of flames after having been pursued at unbelievable speeds.

McQueen, himself a race fan, later starred in the 1970 racing movie *LeMans*. He wanted the chase scene to be as authentic as possible. He certainly succeeded.

With San Francisco streets blocked off by local police, the black Charger, and the green ´68 Mustang GT with McQueen at the wheel, tore through the chase scene. Both vehicles carried in-car cameras that added to the reality of the breathtaking chase.

To film the scene, Warner Brothers purchased a pair of four-speed equipped ´68 Charger R/Ts. Reportedly, Dodge benefited in Charger sales after the movie was screened. McQueen did much of his own high-speed driving.

After speeds in the 100mph range plus crashes onto pavement from spectacular jumps, damage was done to the cars. The special effects during the latter part of the chase had one of the Charger passengers firing a shotgun at the Mustang. The movie's final scene was the total destruction of one of the Chargers as it crashed into a gas station and, unfortunately, was consumed in a ball of fire.

It is one of cinema's all-time classic chase scenes. And a black ´68 Charger R/T was one of the main characters, just behind Steve McQueen and his ´68 Mustang GT.

The movie poster for Dirty Mary Crazy Larry *shows the Charger going up in flames in the background.*

Dirty Mary Crazy Larry

In 1974, the movie with an unlikely title employed a modified, bright-yellow ´69 Charger in lots of mayhem. Starring Peter Fonda and Susan George, the car screamed over country roads and some off roads at out-of-sight speeds.

Three identical Chargers were used in making the movie. One of the stunt cars actually was a ´68 model. Modified with a roll cage, it was used in the more-dangerous high-speed runs.

We are sad to note that one of these Chargers met a death as gruesome as the one in Bullitt. The last scene has the Charger driving into a moving train at high speeds.

It was an amazing bit of movie gimmickry with the Charger. Towed by a rope attached to a pickup—its steering wheel locked—the Charger was towed at about 50 mph. As the train passed between the vehicles, its steel wheels sliced the rope on track. That freed the Charger to slam dramatically into the side of the train as pyro charges were ignited. End of Charger!

This clone Charger was constructed by John Murphy and is identical to the car used in the movie Dirty Mary Crazy Larry.

Fireball 500

This forgotten movie, now almost four decades old, used a vintage Chrysler muscle machine that was hard to recognize in its on-screen appearance.

The "star" of this 1966 flick from American International Pictures was a highly modified ´66 Barracuda. It would have taken a Chrysler expert to identify it. The car's look still makes it a classic rod. Recently, it was reproduced as a die cast model in the

Recognize this early Barracuda? This gutty rod started life as one before being "made up" for the movie **Fireball 500.**

Johnny Lightning series.

The *Fireball 500* car had its standard Barracuda fastback top completely shaved off. From the cowl forward it was white, but red from the cowl on back to the rear. Flames cascaded down two-thirds the length of the body.

The car also sported side exhaust pipes, a Chrysler Hemi engine, small twin windshields, racing mirrors, and exhaust stacks sticking through the hood. "Plymouth" was scripted on the front quarters with Plymouth *Fireball 500* on the front grille.

Guess it's not surprising to learn that hot rod design genius George Barris accomplished the remarkable look.

The movie featured teen movie stars Frankie Avalon and Annette Funicello. The plot involved a promoter who hired a stock car driver for a cross-country race that turned out be a bootlegging run.

Backdraft

One of the big stars of this 1991 movie, which featured Kurt Russell, was a ´71 Plymouth Satellite.

Backdraft *starred Kurt Russell in the 1990s. In it, a ´71 Plymouth Satellite was painted like a Chicago police unit. (Photo courtesy of* **Encyclopedia of American Police Cars***)*

Garbed with the markings of the Chicago Police Department, the Satellite was used in a flashback scene. Russell's father was a Chicago fireman and the car was used to block traffic from running over fire hoses.

Although a 383-cid engine was available for the Satellite, had the movie engine been historically accurate, the cruiser probably would have carried the 225-cid Slant Six engine.

Bad Georgia Road

This movie hit the screen in 1977, with Gary Lockwood and Carol Lynley starring. Maybe getting more attention were the pair of mistreated, muscle-flexing Chryslers. Both cars were ´70 models—a Charger and a Road Runner.

We're talking about another moonshine-running movie and the performance-oriented Chryslers certainly were right for the role. Lots of chase sequences left both machines a little worse for wear.

Randall Waring, a fan of the movie **Vanishing Point,** *worked to clone this ´Cuda to be identical to the movie version. (Randall Waring photo)*

The "Fantasm" movies:

A number of ´71 ´Cudas and ´Cuda look-alikes were used in a series of horror movies that carried the "Fantasm" name. In order to look menacing, all of the machines were painted a cold black. Director Don Coscarelli always liked the ´Cuda from his high school days, so there was no doubt the flashy Chrysler model would be used in his movie.

Vanishing Point

This 1971 flick has become somewhat of a cult movie and modern plastic models of it recently have been produced. This time, a ´70 Challenger was selected for a co-starring position.

Actually, four of the Alpine White cars carried four-speed trannies matched to 440-cid V-8s. One of the cars was an automatic. The latter car never made it onto the screen where lots of chasing, jumping, heavy-duty shocks, and special bracings were added.

Much of the action was filmed in the desert. One of the cars carried cameras on the hood, the front bumper, and the rear bumper. Like the Charger in the *Bullitt* movie, the Challenger met its death crashing at high speeds into a bulldozer.

Duel

It wasn't a very fair duel with a red late-1960s Plymouth Valiant sedan trying to hold off a menacing, vintage Peterbilt tanker truck in a desert confrontation. Dennis Weaver was the driver and ended up the victor, but like many other Chrysler-based movie stars, the red Valiant would be destroyed. It and the tanker dropped over a steep incline and were demolished.

Fast and Furious

There are two versions of the *Fast and Furious* movies. The first version used a single Hemi Charger, while the second version used a number of Challengers.

Blade

This Wesley Snipes movie used a ´69 Charger R/T as one of its main characters.

Two Lane Blacktop

Although there wasn't a classic Chrysler vehicle in a lead role, this popular movie featured a light-colored, winged Charger Daytona in a cameo role.

The Fast and Furious *Hemi Charger by Revell. (Courtesy of Revell-Monogram)*

TV Shows

This ´71 Challenger, from the "Mod Squad" TV show, was converted to look like a ´72, when no rag-tops were built. (Greg Weber photo)

"The Mod Squad"

It was a two-guys-and-a-girl weekly hit show. They were hip and free-spirited like that era. And as part of the trend, a tough Chrysler hauler also performed before the camera.

The model of choice here was a ´71 Challenger convertible, which had been professionally modified to look like a ´72 model—a year that was void of ragtops. George Barris again made the modification.

Interestingly, the car was located in a woeful condition almost two decades later. It was then restored to its original GY8 Gold Metallic color. Power came from a 340-cid, four-barrel mill with Chrysler's famed 727 TorqueFlite automatic.

Reportedly, there were three of the gold and black-striped Challengers. Two of them probably appeared later in a low-budget flick called *Group Marriage*. The restored Challenger remains in the proud possession of Floridian Greg Weber.

"The Dukes of Hazzard"

The Charger, the star of this backwoods-based show, could well have been the most recognizable Dodge muscle car in history. Generations have watched the show and the antics that a fleet of orange ´69 Chargers performed.

A point must be made about this car before going any further. Certainly, many more than one of the Chargers were used. Some of the tricks performed with the cars ended their TV performing careers.

They all were known as the "General Lee," and to be exact, they were Charger R/Ts. At least that's what they were before they were bought by Warner Brothers Television. The exact number of the cars isn't known, but it was a bunch!

Some interesting equipment installed on the cars included a horn that tooted the first dozen notes of "Dixie," along with a stout roll cage inside the driver's compartment. The Chargers had automatic transmissions, and their power plants were equipped with aluminum intake manifolds.

The stock frames were weighted at four strategic

One of the original Dodge Chargers prepared to star with Bo, Luke, and Daisy and their television adventures. (OCW photo)

The "General Lee" Charger is just as popular in the 21st century as evidenced by this replica model.

Bo and Luke Duke never wasted time opening the door of the "General Lee." They entered the ´69 Charger the NASCAR way! (OCW photo)

points, and were fitted with gas shock absorbers to keep the car level during the jump landings. The cars also carried 30-inch glass pack mufflers that made a cool sound. Their Shelby rims held new radial tires with special inner-tube inserts.

The big change in looks, though, was the flashy orange paint job with a Confederate flag on the roof and a stock car-type "01" on the sides of both doors. Speaking of the doors—they never were opened during the series. Luke and Bo entered and exited the "General Lee" Charger over the door NASCAR style.

Tom Wopat, who played Luke Duke, has fond memories about that special fleet of Dodges.

"Boy, we wrecked a bunch of them during the years of the show," he said. "I think that we went through more than one of them per show."

Wopat said skilled stunt drivers did most of the wild tricks with the Chargers, but both he and co-star John Schneider also did their share of the less-dangerous tricks.

"Both John and I knew how to slide the cars around. We did a lot of those dust-raising stops and screeching exits. I did smack into a semi-truck one time, and John ran into a couple of buildings."

Sonny Shroyer, who played the numb-brained deputy, also said that he wheeled the Hazzard County police cars on occasion when chasing the General Lees.

"One time, I lost control of the car, ran over a fence and into a ravine. It wasn't planned, but they got in on film and used it," Sonny explained.

Some of the old General Lees still are around, along with many more clones of the famous Chargers. It will be a long time before the these orange Chargers are forgotten!

"Adam-12"

One of the greatest producers of TV police shows during the 1960s was Jack Webb, with his "Dragnet," and later "Adam-12."

That latter show was based on a pair of young police officers and their daily duties as patrolmen for the Los Angeles Police Department. Starring Martin Milner and Kent McCord, the show lasted from 1968 through 1975, and remains a classic in reruns today.

Much of the show was shot when the pair were in their cruiser. For the first year that car was a ´67

The popularity of the "General Lee" Charger has resulted in a significant number of clones, such as this example.

Plymouth Belvedere. "Adam 12" also used ´68 and ´69 Belvederes, ´71 Plymouth Satellites, and finally, 1972 AMC Matadors.

"Nash Bridges"

Don Johnson is the star of this action TV program which started in the mid-1990s. A ´71 ´Cuda was the star of the show. Actually, it was a ´70 Cuda made to look one year newer. In fact, there were three ´70s that received the modification. They all carried a Chrysler 340-cid power plant.

Initially, the stock Lemon Twist color was selected, but it was decided the color wouldn't show up that well on camera, so a darker color was selected.

Alan Foxx explained that his company—Ultimate Rides in El Paso, Texas—was responsible for the cars. A 440-cid V-8 car was also constructed. It certainly had a lot more power than the 340-cid cars.

When the program was cancelled, all the cars were auctioned off. One of them drew an amazing six-figure price at auction!

Other TV Programs

A number of other popular shows used the ever-available Chrysler models including "The Brady Bunch" (´Cudas), "Mannix" (´70 and ´71 ´Cudas), "Medical Center" (Challengers) and probably others.

Police Vehicles

With machines with the performance caliber of the subject Dodges and Plymouths, it's not surprising that a large number of them would find themselves wearing the black and white of real police vehicles and not coated with wild Chrysler colors.

A number of models were selected for this duty, including the 1967 Plymouth Belvedere. An issue of *Mopar Muscle* described it this way: "... a base model Belvedere concealed a pure muscle car, a Clark Kent body and a Superman spirit—or more accurately, a 'mom and pop' car with the heart of a GTX."

Not available to the buying public, these Plymouth police cars couldn't be ordered by the buying public until they were pretty well used up by the law.

The special models carried 14 x 5 1/2 wheels, a 70-amp battery, a 46-amp alternator, plus a stiffer police suspension system consisting of heavy-duty rear springs, torsion bars, shocks, and an anti-sway bar.

In order to outrun the street versions of this hauler, the Plymouth Division installed the 383 Commando high-performance package rated at 325 hp and 425 lb-ft of torque. Compression was set at 10 to 1 with a huge Carter four-barrel carburetor, dual exhausts, and Hemi-style mufflers.

With a 3.23 rear end ratio, it was a compromise between acceleration and high speed chasing. Reportedly, these models had a top speed of nearly 130 mph.

In 1969, the Dodge Coronet also was a popular police model. Practically devoid of trim, it carried the 383-cid high-performance V-8 rated at 330 hp this model year. Reportedly, these cars had about a 15 mph higher top speed than the standard street versions. The Los Angeles Police Department was a heavy user of these machines.

Many of these Dodge police cruisers came with a rear sway bar which almost completely eliminated understeer at all speeds and made the model extremely nimble.

In 1970, both the Dodge Coronet and Plymouth Belvedere were popular police choices. And just as was the case with the general public, the Dodge's wild, flared front end treatment was an object of love or hate by the men in blue.

The ´71 Coronet was used by a number of local and state police units. A number of engines were available, including the longstanding 383-cid engine, and versions of the 340- and 360-cid V-8 mills.

Through the years, a number of these cars have been bought at sales and restored to their police configurations. A number of these restorations have been accomplished by the same officers who were behind the wheel of the mighty Mopars on official duty.

A 1974 Dodge Monaco Mt. Pleasant, Illinois, police car appeared in the Blues Brothers *movie as the "Bluesmobile." (Photo courtesy of* Encyclopedia of American Police Cars*)*

This ´75 Plymouth Fury is from TV's "Hill Street Blues." Portions of the TV show actually were shot in the Chicago area. (Photo courtesy of Encyclopedia of American Police Cars*)*

Chapter Nine: The Fading Muscle Car Glow

While performance was waning in 1973 and beyond, the unmistakable looks of the Chrysler muscle cars continued in varying degrees, even though the era of mega-horsepower and brute muscle was vanishing. A vivid example of how much performance had disappeared is the fact that Plymouth stopped publishing horsepower figures in 1975.

Let's look at the muscular Mopars model by model and see how some faded away, while others "dusted off" the performance and appearance turndown, at least for a while.

Plymouth Road Runner

Still looking like a "Runner," the ´73 model didn´t change very much, even while other cars were emerging from the muscle image.

The Road Runner's grille received an update and the hood bulge featured a pair of triangular cut-outs. A stripe curved down the body side and then climbed the rear pillar, finally meeting its opposite number over the roof.

The standard engine was a weaker 318-cid V-8 with only 170 net hp. A version of the 440-cid produced 280 hp.

The ´74 Road Runner was almost identical to the previous model, but that year the 360-cid V-8 became standard. The top 275-hp, 440-cid V-8 was still available, but only 79 were built. Brazen performance was getting to be a bad word.

The Fury platform was the base for the 1975 edition—still called the Road Runner. Now, a 400-cid V-8 was the top engine. In 1976, the Road Runner was downsized—becoming an option for Volaré buyers.

While one might have thought this change would have spelled "boring," it wasn't the case. The Road Runner identification was on the sheet metal with the name spelled out across the bottom of the door. A $300 appearance package called the "Super Pak" added spoilers, flares, and window louvers.

The ´78 Road Runner again looked good with multi-colored striping, lower-case door lettering, and integral

The dramatic hood treatment on this ´74 Road Runner holds up the standards of the earlier performance models.

The ´74 Road Runner design and detailing certainly hasn't lost anything. Seeing one of these models is rare these days.

Horses were down in 1974, but this four-barrel 360 mill could get the job done in this watered-down performance era.

Check out the nifty louvers on this 1978 Road Runner.

window louvers. In 1980, the Plymouth Division gave up the ghost and the fabulous Road Runner name was gone.

Plymouth Barracuda

The 1973 Barracuda still looked just about the same as its powerful muscle car cousins. Striping was similar, with the only differences being front and rear bumper guards. It was similar for the ´74 Cuda. It was the final edition, but it still looked bitchin', to say the least.

The ´74 ´Cuda´s body style had a style similar to previous models but the side body stripe was considerably different.

Dodge Challenger

Style and performance weren't a big part of the Challenger for the last two years (1973 and ´74) of its

The displacement-model badge for the '74 was identical to those used during the Mopar muscle era.

This ´74 Challenger's hood was done after the performance era was gone, but Mopar still was showing its design stuff.

This ´74 Challenger shows an interesting treatment. Four stacked stripes started as solid lines and ended as angled lines.

Dodge Charger

In 1973, a subtle change was made to the Charger line. There was a new grille and taillight design, but performance was being de-emphasized. Now, comfort and luxury were the design priorities. A wide mid-body stripe reached almost the complete length of the car.

The curb weight of the ´74 Charger was now more than 4,000 pounds, and while the weight increased, the power continued to decline. Certainly not what you could do to make performance. Yet it was just fine for luxury. No longer were racing stripes or bulging hoods available. They weren't in the scheme of things.

1978 would be the final year for the once-vaunted existence. Both the convertible and big block now were history.

Certainly, nothing significant was changed on the ´73 Challenger. The model was almost identical to the previous year, with the exception of the larger bumper pads. Of course, under the hood the once awesome horsepower was quickly disappearing.

Without a whimper, the nifty Challenger went away with the 1974 model. It still looked stunning with the same basic body shape. What a pity to see it go, but the buying public had turned against everything the Challenger stood for.

The famed R/T still was in place on the ´73 Charger R/T. To some, it looked better than the earlier versions.

The '74 Charger had an interesting stripe option which varied in width throughout its total body length.

Dodge applied the Daytona name to a '77 Charger. Note the wide body stripe that started on each end but never met.

Charger. The Magnum carried on for 1979. It was a model that was basically a Charger with a sloping nose—which might have pointed to its return to big-time stock car racing. But it's well known, this wouldn't happen for many years to come.

Dodge Dart

A Dart Sport Rallye was introduced for 1973. Although the performance had been chiseled away, there still was some Dodge pizzazz.

There was the patented stripe that started atop the front fenders and then swept up the rear pillar and over the roof. Going back to an old racing habit, the "Dodge" name was lettered across the rear quarters.

The '73 Twister package sported non-functional hood scoops and a blacked-out hood, just like the good old days.

The Dart kept its popularity through 1975, retaining the same basic body lines and a relatively-potent small block. It was Dodge's top selling model during the period.

Also for the 1974-'75 model years, there was a huge design bump with the so-called "Dart Hang 10," which was identified by option code A63.

It was trendy with a definite California flair—Spinnaker White color, twin hood scoops, the hint of a

The Duster changed very little through the mid-'70s, as this '73 model demonstrates.

surfboard on its hood, and about the wildest blue-and-orange striping and decals you can remember. Blue and orange accents were also carried through in the interior. A 360-cid V-8 was the biggest engine available.

As most of you know, the "Hang 10" moniker has a surfing connotation. The fold-down rear seat was supposedly fashioned so surfboards could lay through the car unobstructed.

Dodge Super Coupe

In 1976, with styling and performance dropping off the kitchen table across the American car industry, Dodge surprised with its so-called R/T Super Coupe. It was part of the mid-size intermediate Aspen line, but there definitely was a genealogy connected to the Dart.

The Coupe sported a unique body-length stripe, rear spoiler, rear window louvers, and a front spoiler.

For a muscle look in the Bicentennial year, this was about as good as it got.

The late '70s Dodge Aspen Super Coupe had no muscle but the 1960s and early '70s performance look was there.

A mid-'70s special edition was called the Dart "Hang 10." This rare car had California surfing written all over it.

Chapter Ten: Checkered Flags and Chrysler's Racing Muscle

Much of the Mopar mystique in the golden era of muscle cars had a direct association with racing. The models had the racing look—with their swooping designs, sporty striping, and the performance aspects of the era's racing machines. When these Chrysler-made haulers hit the track in race trim, they showed their prowess big time.

The company advertised its success on the race track, both in oval and drag racing. They felt the checkered flags meant a lot in the dealer showrooms. And Chrysler executives certainly wanted to make sure the Dodge and Plymouth model names were in place on their race vehicles for all to see. It just made marketing sense for that era.

The models were receiving attention and the king of the Chrysler Corporation's engine family, the Hemi, monopolized whatever motor sport it entered. Its racing success also was used in any advertising campaigns for models that were powered by the giant mill.

Chrysler also carried the racing connections directly to the names of particular models.

Race Name Association

First, there was the NASCAR connection. Three Chrysler models were "Holmogated"—made NASCAR-legal by building a specified number of the model for the public. They were run in Winston Cup competition. The models were the Charger 500, and the two winged machines, the Dodge Charger Daytona and the Plymouth Road Runner Superbird.

Chrysler, like other auto manufacturers of the period, associated their cars with racing. Several models used the R/T designation—as in the magazine *Road and Track*. And there was the Dodge Dart GTS, the Plymouth Barracuda Formula S, the Satellite Sebring, the Coronet 500, and the Plymouth GTX.

Some of these names, like Sebring or 500, suggested a race or race track. "Formula" suggested a type of racing. Many car manufacturers used the GT shorthand, which stood for "gran turismo"—Italian for "grand touring," a class of road racing.

The race connections definitely were working, so why not continue to use them?

The Race Look

These Chrysler machines had the look, and then some! In fact, some looked like they were roaring along just sitting there!

The racing look was personified by the Dodge Charger Daytona and Plymouth Road Runner Superbird, whose design was derived from wind tunnel calculations.

Their razor-edge grille sliced through the air, and along with that aerodynamic advantage was a body design that could be competitive in the 21st century. There also were a number of wingless Charger models that would make themselves felt on the racetrack.

Several of the Dodge and Plymouth models led the

way with the race look by including hood pins. Many Mopar performance models carried them as options.

Actually, there were two different versions of pin placement. Some models used a pair of them on the front edge of the hood. Another interesting variation used four pins that required the complete hood to be lifted off, drag racing style.

Certain Dodge R/T models carried appearance-only scoops on the forward section of their rear-quarter panels. The rare ´70 Charger R/Ts toted a large, nonfunctional vertical scoop that was located just forward of the front door crease.

The ´67 Dodge Coronet R/T showed its full racing colors with a pair of stacked scoops just behind the door handle.

One of the greatest assets in oval track racing is

With two race versions in the SCCA Trans Am series, it's not surprising T/A was a model name of one of the cars.

Ever seen a pure race car that didn't sport hood pins? They were popular on Dodges and Plymouths during this performance era.

It didn't look like a street car appendage but the spoiler worked great on the NASCAR, USAC, and ARCA racetracks.

aerodynamic down force. In effect, it pushes down on the rear of the body and increases traction. In the 1960s, various racing experiments proved its worthiness.

Chrysler noticed that rear trunk design could be used to aid in this phenomenon. It was applied to the ´69 Charger and Charger 500 models. They became the earliest street cars to demonstrate the advantages of the rear deck spoiler design.

It was accomplished with a slight "kick up" on the back edge of the rear deck. Granted, there probably was little down force provided by this appendage, but it gave the look of a NASCAR racer.

Both the AAR ´Cuda and Challenger T/A went even further, using small, attached triangular rear deck spoilers and the exhausts that protruded in front of the rear wheel.

Later, Chrysler products of the muscle car period also demonstrated significant flares on all four wheel openings. In actual race cars, where such flares are common, they're used to encase the wider racing tires. They weren't needed for wider tires on these consumer vehicles, but they looked "racing cool."

Carrying that concept to the next level were the rear-deck-mounted "Go Wings," available on a number of Chrysler produced models of that era.

At legal highway speeds, it's doubtful the "Go Wings" provided much advantage, but they definitely provided the racing look! The wings were available on

A ´64 Dodge MAX WEDGE HT, The race-inspired slanted roof and powerful Max Wedge engine made the no-nonsense ´64 Dodge a popular choice for racing. (Angelo Van Bogart/OCW)

Even the "GT" on this Dodge Dart GTS brings up thoughts of winding "gran turismo" road race courses.

The ´70 Coronet R/T sported this macho racing scoop just forward of the rear wheel opening.

What's the most famous number in racing? It's "500"—Indy and Daytona—and the Charger 500. (Michael Smith Photo)

This ´69 Dodge Super Bee had a pro stock-style hood. The four pins could be released and the hood lifted, drag race-style.

A recognizable race car characteristic is flaired wheel wells to accomodate wide tires—modeled on this ´71 Road Runner.

certain models of Chargers, Challengers and some other Chrysler-made cars.

The variety of scooped hoods that were so abundant at this time, had a macho performance look that also gave the race appearance. Most of the hood scoops were nonfunctional and were strictly for looks. A few actually funneled the cool air into the carburetor, or carburetors.

Front end aerodynamics, with the exception of the Daytona and Superbird, wasn't seriously considered. These cars had flat vertical front ends that stopped the air like a barn door. Some of the first under-grille spoilers came along during this period, with the winged cars and others getting them as an option.

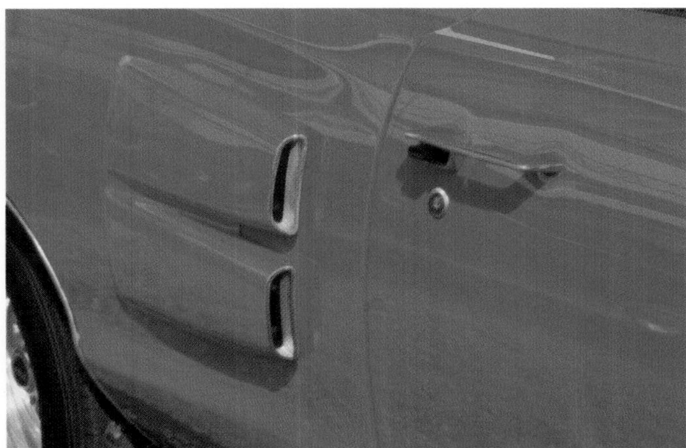

Twin racing-style scoops were popular in this era, as seen by this rear-quarter pair.

The race look even was carried to the gas cap on certain models. The earliest to feature this was the ´66 Charger. The chrome-and-black design looked like it should be resting on the deck of a road racing machine. Later, the winged cars also sported a similar gas cap design.

Of course, what would a racing look be without racing stripes? Many of these Mopar models used them to the hilt, with the most common use being the twin parallel striping across the rear deck.

NASCAR Grand National (Today's Winston Cup)

It's great if you've got a hot-looking model, but if it can´t get it done on the racetrack, you've lost a tremendous advertising edge.

The late 1960s were an exciting time on the racetracks, as well as in the muscle car hobby. Chrysler, along with the other manufacturers, was certain that a checkered flag during a NASCAR race would bring potential customers into their dealerships. And the cars that were competing were a lot closer to their street brothers than they are today.

That situation was particularly the case with three Chrysler creations of the late 1960s.

The Charger 500 was the first. It didn't perform particularly well, but the later winged cars tore up the competition. In fact, they did so well they would quickly be ruled ineligible.

Chrysler wanted to win NASCAR in the worst way. And the company thought it had the answer with the swoopy ´68 Charger. It proved not to be up to its performance on the street. In fact, in the 49 races it ran that model year, it only took the checkered flag five times. The year before, Dodge and Plymouth had it all their own way, winning three-dozen times out of only 49 outings.

The 1967 Grand National season winner was, not unexpectedly, the "King"—Richard Petty. He won it in a Plymouth Satellite Hemi. The company played up the accomplishment to the hilt in its national advertising. The Plymouth name was scripted prominently on the rear quarters for all to see.

This rear deck spoiler was a popular option that often was seen on a variety of Mopar models.

There's an interesting story about how that Satellite actually became a race car. It was delivered to Petty's racing facility in a so-called stripped-out "Body in White" configuration.

Translated, that means it carried race-type suspension with beefy leaf springs in the rear and torsion bars in place on the front. Unlike the supposedly stock cars of today that are specially prepared and are quite distant from production versions, Petty's Satellite body was 99 percent factory stock!

The Charger, with its excellent aerodynamics, became the standard Dodge race model in 1968. Looks certainly were deceiving with the ´68 Charger. Its design made it look like it could fly like the wind. But two of its most popular body design features actually contributed to its poor performance.

One was its nifty, recessed grille design that caused air to mound up, creating drag. The tunneled slope of the rear window created turbulence at high speeds which slowed down the Charger. There had to be some changes made, and quickly, to be able to compete with the more slippery-bodied NASCAR opposition.

This ´70 R/T shows racing-style hood scoops above a 440 Six Pack power plant that lies just underneath.

A change was needed quickly so the Dodge Division designed the low-production Charger 500. Dodge called on an aftermarket company called Creative Industries to incorporate some drag-reducing modifications to the original ´68 Charger R/T design. One change was the grille, actually using one from a ´68 Coronet. The angle of the rear window also was changed and the Charger 500 gained about 10 mph of additional top speed over the previous racing model Charger.

In effect, the Charger 500 was the first pure factory effort to produce a model for race competition. Even with the changes, the Charger 500 still couldn't keep up with the Ford competitors.

To qualify for racing competition, NASCAR decreed that at least 500 of the model had to be produced. The racing body called this the "Holmogation process."

Three-hundred-ninety-two seems to be the standard number quoted for the Charger 500. That's certainly less than the magic 500 number, but somehow the Charger 500 was allowed to run. Guess it's easy to understand why these Coronet-grilled, rear window altered versions of the ´68 Charger—complete with a '500' numeral displayed in the rear-quarter stripes—are so rare.

The Charger 500s had an interesting array of options in their street versions. First of all, the street versions could be acquired with either the Hemi(the only engine in the race versions) or the 375-hp 440 Magnum engine.

The 500s retained the Charger R/T´s suspension

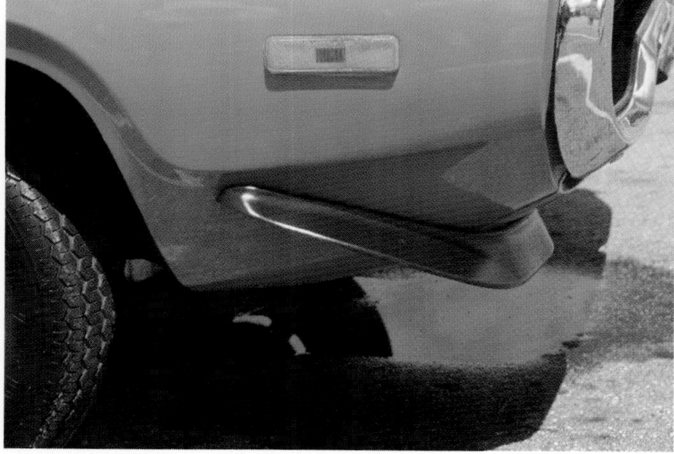

There was also a front spoiler option, shown on this ´72 Plymouth Satellite Sebring.

This ´66 Dodge Charger displays its race-inspired gas cap.

The term "racing" usually goes with the word "stripe" and that sure is the case with this red-striped ´68 Dodge GTS.

system which mounted heavy-duty springs and shocks, beefy torsion bars, and a large front sway bar. Transmission choices were either the TorqueFlite automatic or the four-speed. There also was that hint of an integral rear spoiler.

From an advertising point-of-view, there wasn't much to cheer about from the corporate offices. But this updated Charger would begin to change everything, bringing Dodge closer to the front of the pack in NASCAR racing.

The next mutation was even more dramatic. While this version's official name was the Charger Daytona, the Charger portion of the name never got much mention. To every Mopar fan, it was the Daytona, a name and a concept that immediately brought attention to one of the wildest looking machines to ever take the track or street.

It's interesting how this winged warrior often was accepted both at the dealership and on the track. Reactions were entirely different. On the track, especially the longer NASCAR ovals, it was unbeatable. The Charger Daytona was a fantasy of power and aerodynamics.

For some reason, the dramatic change brought a lack of interest from the buying public. The models sat in dealership lots, many of them unsold. Some were there for as much as a year.

In order to sell the Daytona—and its look-alike Plymouth version, the Superbird—sometimes it was necessary to remove the tall tail and substitute a stock front-end for the pointed nose cone.

The attention the models got on the racetrack was

The '71 Charger R/T could be equipped with exhaust tips that had a racing look.

Before the Daytona, there was the Dodge Charger 500. It looked good, but its on-track performance wasn't effective.

Awesome Richard Petty drove this Hemi Satellite to many 1967 wins. Its "Plymouth" lettering clearly was visible. (Mike Slade Photo)

There's been nothing like these "tailfeathers!" Richard Petty agrees, the wing revolutionized NASCAR while it was legal. (John Carollo Photo)

well worth the effort to build them. The Ford competition didn't have anything close to the "wildness factor" of these models. The winged warriors blew away Ford's and its Torino-based Talladega and Mercury Cyclone Spoiler II models. Even these slick machines couldn't compare with the down force provided by the Daytona and Superbird.

Rest assured, the wing and pointed nose did perform their intended purpose. The overhead wing on those models produced tremendous down force and the front end at racing speed reduced lift to about 1/10th the value of a traditional nose. The Daytona, which came first in 1969, won about 80 percent of the races it entered, including 22 NASCAR Grand National competitions.

In 1970, a Charger Daytona with NASCAR driver Bobby Isaacs at the wheel turned in a closed-course record speed of 201.104 mph at the Talladega Speedway. Chrysler made the most of the accomplishment in the national media. The winged models also have run at the Bonneville Salt Flats and showed exceptional speed with modified power plants.

Only 503 Daytonas were built for the 1969 model year, but they continued into the 1970 season with NASCAR. Also, the Daytonas continued to get additional national attention with success in both the USAC and ARCA circuits.

The 1970 season saw the Plymouth Road Runner Superbird come on strong with 21 wins. The ´69 Daytonas still were running and came up with just four fewer victories. It was definitely a Chrysler show at the finish lines and winner's circle!

It was all too much for NASCAR which always is looking for equality on the track. As a result, the winged Chrysler-made vehicles, plus two Ford-produced cars, were excluded from further competition in their current garb for the 1971 season.

In addition, the equally wild horsepower race among major automakers was reigned in by NASCAR. It legislated that the engine displacement of the Hemi and other racing engines would have to be greatly reduced for competition. The NASCAR standard was reduced to only 305 cid, making the magnificent Chrysler Hemi models and others noncompetitive.

One of the most successful Superbirds was driven by Ramo Stott at the A.R.C.A. (Automobile Racing Club of America) circuit. He was happy to recall the way the machine handled on the track. "You could really feel the effects of that rear wing which started working when you got up to about 100 mph. It really planted the car on the track. We normally set the spoiler angle at five-

The front of the ´69 Dodge Charger was altered to make it more aerodynamic on the NASCAR circuit. (OCW photo)

The rear window and roofline were altered as well on the ´69 Charger 500 to increase aerodynamics. (OCW photo)

You didn't need to say a particular NASCAR car had a Hemi engine. The 426 cid figure was all that needed to be said.

Country legend Marty Robbins also was an impressive NASCAR racer. His #42 1971 Charger's paint scheme was unforgettable.

to-seven degrees," he adds.

"I remember one time at Talladega when I got the car off the track at about 200 mph. I just straightened out the front of the car and it stabilized and came back onto the track completely straight. As I think about it, that wing was a real safety device."

Ernie Derr—biggest winner in U.S. stock car racing—takes his 8th IMCA Stock Car Championship in a Champion-fitted Dodge

In 1967–ARCA, IMCA and USAC stock car racing bowed to "Dodge Fever." And Champion sparked it. It's more proof that Champion spark plugs give outstanding performance! Why should you settle for less?

Champion spark plugs . . . the heart of a tune-up

CHAMPION SPARK PLUG COMPANY • TOLEDO, OHIO 43601

Ernie Derr and his Dodges became legendary in regional dirt track racing in the 1960s. (1966 Champion Spark Plug ad)

The "Winged Warriors" slipped into obscurity, but during their brief, fantastic era on the NASCAR ovals, Chrysler's Dodge and Plymouth Divisions enjoyed a huge publicity benefit. There probably never will be anything like them again!

Dodge used its racetrack success to publicize its muscle models. With national advertisements, drivers like two-time USAC Stock Car champ and Charger racer Don White and Daytona NASCAR racer Bobby Isaacs proclaimed the virtues of the street versions of their racing machines.

Of the Charger R/T, White said: "It's one of the greatest buys a true performance-minded guy could find anywhere." Added Isaacs about the Daytona: "It's got a snout that sticks out a country mile, and an adjustable spoiler that looks two-stories tall in the rear."

The Chrysler-produced Dodges and Plymouths were terrors of the NASCAR ovals and often flexed their muscle as they took a lion's share of checkered flags.

Mopar Dirt Stock Cars

Dirt stock car driver Ernie Derr might not have the national recognition of a Richard Petty, but with a Dodge Charger, the Iowa driver became king of the dirt tracks.

Ernie started his "Dodge Rebellion" with the reintroduction of the Hemi engine in 1964. His career

Typical Hemi engine set-up for a NASCAR-style stock car. The powerplant really monopolized the competition.

began in 1950 and included some racing with the first Chrysler Hemi in the mid-1950s. Derr had over 250 wins and 120 second places!

He's best known, though, for his orange Chargers. They won the IMCA (International Motor Contest Association) championships each year from 1966 through 1971. His old 1970 Dodge is still around. Its owners don't want to restore it and leave it exactly like it was, complete with all its "beat and bang" marks.

Plymouth happily used Richard Petty's NASCAR success to advertise in performance oriented magazines like Hot Rod in 1966. (Plymouth advertisement)

Sunday Driver.

Richard Petty does his most spectacular driving on Sunday afternoons. Since the '66 NASCAR season opened, Petty and his Hemi-engined Plymouth Belvedere have rewritten the qualifying lap records on just about every track in the Grand National circuit. And first place in this year's Daytona "500" went to Petty with an all-time race record average of 160.625 mph. Of course, Petty's Hemi Belvedere isn't for sale at your Plymouth Dealer's . . . even if you wanted one. It was built just for racing.

But Petty races a Plymouth for a lot of the same reasons so many people buy the production version of the Plymouth. Things like torsion-bar front suspension. Asymmetrical rear springs. And a complete package of safety features like safety door handles . . . all standard equipment. And options like disc brakes, heavy-duty suspension, limited-slip differential and a choice of engines on up to the street version of the 426 Hemi. And the same history of reliability that makes the race car a winner. So see your Plymouth Dealer and check out one of the '66 Plymouths . . . they're winners Monday through Saturday too.

PLYMOUTH DIVISION

Plymouth ...a great car by Chrysler Corporation.

Richard Petty became a NASCAR legend for his "Sunday driving" and famous for his number 43 Plymouth. (Plymouth advertisement)

USAC superstar Roger McCluskey is shown at speed in his Plymouth, running on dirt. (USAC photo)

WINGED DODGES & PLYMOUTHS

The Brief but Glorious Flight of the Winged Warriors

The ultimate in spoilers were the winged Charger Daytona and Road Runner Superbird machines. Their body-colored, high-mounted wings were attached to the cars on the flat tops of the rear fenders. There was no denying their link to racing!

And it goes without saying the wings were installed primarily for race use as these cars went on the NASCAR circuit. A rare few went to the streets, practically in race trim.

The tall-standing airfoils worked on the Daytonas and Superbirds but you needed to double the speed limit before they started to react. That was good for racing, but not too practical on the interstate!

All the winged cars used the Hemi power plant in racing competition. The winged cars also were available with four-barrel and "Six Pack" 440-cid engines. But to prove that these models were built to move to the racetrack with only minimal changes, street models couldn't be purchased with vinyl roof, air conditioning, sunroof, luggage rack, or two-tone paint.

Chrysler Corporation tested modifications in these "birds" for the 1970 model year. Using a more attractive and rakish body shell, several designs were tested including bi- and tri-winged scale models. The wings tested were of varied widths.

Different nose cones also were tested in the Wichita State University wind tunnel early in 1970. While the redesigned winged Chryslers would have been great looking cars, NASCAR prohibitions ended this brief design exercise. Chrysler and Ford, in particular, went in new directions. The winged Chryslers are memorable and very collectible vehicles today!

There is an interesting sidelight to this single-year winged car. Rumors persist that three 1970 Dodge Charger Daytonas were built. One was pictured, along with specs, on the 1970 Dodge Scat Pack brochure. Externally, the car looked very similar to the ´69 original, though appeared to have cleaner aerodynamics, especially the front end. Whatever the effort, it didn't amount to a second production Daytona built for the 1970 model year. Also, there was some indication Dodge considered building a Daytona for the 1971 model year. Research was conducted by Chrysler Corporation at Wichita State University in the first quarter of 1970. It concentrated on various designs intended to

While a revised 1970 Charger Daytona was featured in this 1970 Dodge "Scat Pack" promotion, it never was sold to the public. (Dodge advertisememt)

Bobby Isaacs tests Charger Daytona:
He drives a winner.

"Well, there's one obvious thing about Charger Daytona. Nobody, but no-ody, walks by without breaking his eck to take a second look. This is the lightly civilized version of the shark-ose built specifically for the long ASCAR ovals. Old Slippery has a nout that strikes out a country mile front, and an adjustable spoiler that ooks two stories tall in the rear. Stan-ard mill is the 440 Magnum but the ne I tested packed the optional street version of the 426 Hemi. Now the Hemi may idle like a coffee can full of rocks, and it may need a wrench applied a little more often than usual. On the other hand, as far as acceleration is concerned, the Hemi turns on where the others shut off. The heavy-duty Rallye Suspension is firm. The test car exhibited moderate understeer under hard driving . . . but there's plenty of torque to break the rear end loose if you have the foot for it.

"Inside, the NASCAR heritage is obvious only in the full-dash equipment. The buckets fit well. Visibility is excellent in the front, not so hot to the rear due to the rear quarter fairings. The standard and heavy-duty rear drums are solid and reliable. You can put down your non-performance friends by pointing out that you have carpeting, disappearing headlights, and a car that you'll never lose in a crowded parking lot."

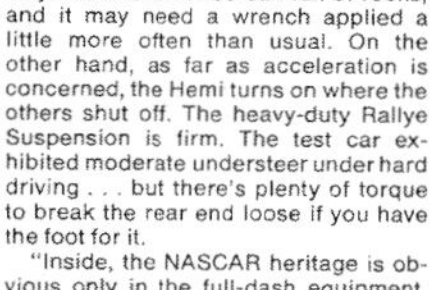

Dodge Charger Daytona
DIMENSIONS

WIDTH	
Track, front	59.7
Track, rear	59.2
Maximum overall car width	76.6
LENGTH	
Wheelbase	117
Overall car length	208.5
HEIGHT	
Overall height	53.0
FRONT COMPARTMENT	
Effective headroom	37.4
Maximum eff. legroom, accelerator	41.4
Shoulder room	58.1
Hiproom	60.6
REAR COMPARTMENT	
Effective headroom	36.4
Minimum eff. legroom	34.1
Rear comp. room	25.3
Shoulder room	58.1
Hiproom	60.4
CAPACITIES	
No. of passengers	5
Fuel tank, gal.	19
Crankcase, qt.	4 (5 when replacing oil filter)
CHASSIS/SUSPENSION	
Body/frame type	unitized
Front suspension	torsion bars
Rear suspension	asymmetrical leaf springs
Steering system	recirculation ball gear
BRAKES—DRUM	
Heavy-duty brakes, standard, (automatic adjusting)	
Front	11 x 3
Rear	11 x 2½
WHEELS/TIRES	
Wheels	14 x 6.0JJ
Tires	F70 x 14 whitewall
ENGINE	
Type and no. of cyls.	V8
Bore and stroke	4.32 x 3.75
Displacement, cu.-in.	440
Compression ratio	9.7:1
Fuel req.	premium
Rated BHP @ RPM	375 @ 4600
Rated torque (lbs./ft. RPM)	480 @ 3200
Carburetion	Carter 4-BBL
Valve train	Hydraulic lifters, pushrods and overhead rocker arms
Cam timing	
Intake duration	268°
Exhaust duration	284°
Exhaust system	dual
DRIVE TRAIN	
Transmission type	3-speed TorqueFlite automatic
Gear ratios	1st 2.45:1
2nd	1.45:1
3rd	1.00:1
Rev.	2.20:1

The only additional item of optional equipment on the Charger Daytona tested by Bobby Isaacs was a set of road wheels.

Dodge published information and photos about the ´70 Charger Daytona in this October 1969 ad but the car wasn't available. (Dodge advertisement)

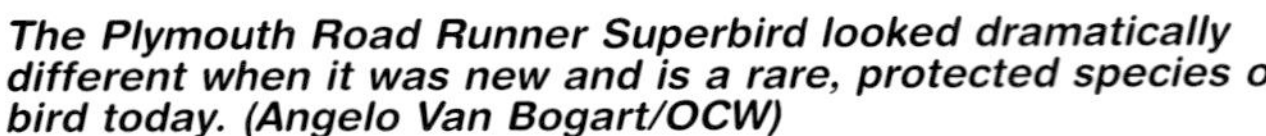

The Plymouth Road Runner Superbird looked dramatically different when it was new and is a rare, protected species of bird today. (Angelo Van Bogart/OCW)

Carefully preserved, this stunning 1970 Plymouth Superbird still turns heads wherever it goes. (OCW)

optimize the nose and wings for more aerodynamic efficiency. By the end of 1970, it was obvious that with NASCAR defrocking the winged machines, a ´71 Daytona just wasn't going to happen.

Mopar winged expert Gary Beineke didn't let that stop him. He actually constructed his Daytona based on the factory report that evolved from the research.

An interesting situation took place in 1969 when Plymouth didn't have a winged vehicle similar to the Dodge Daytona. Richard Petty jumped to Ford. To stay in the racing and publicity game, Plymouth had to do something—quickly!

One might have thought the pair of winged models were close to identical, but that didn't prove to be the case. The Plymouth engineers benefited from problems encountered in the Daytona. But looking at the pair quickly, it was hard to tell the difference.

Plymouth's Road Runner Superbird was designed with a higher angle, which reduced drag. Coronet front fenders and a modified hood were used instead of the Daytona model's Charger pieces. The "Bird" came with a stock vinyl top and there also was a bubble rear window. The Superbird's wing supports were angled more than the Daytona and the wing was a more efficient piece.

The "winged birds" took flight ever so briefly but dominated NASCAR during their stay and left an indelible image in the minds of both Chrysler fans and NASCAR racing devotees everywhere.

NASCAR/ARCA racer Ramo Stott wheeled this potent Superbird #7 to several wins. It's a sharp machine, to be sure!

CHRYSLER'S INDY PACE CARS

One of the greatest exposures for a new model in a race environment often has been its selection as pace car for the Indy 500. Chrysler models got the honor twice during this era with the 1965 Plymouth Sport Fury and the ´71 Dodge Challenger.

1965 Plymouth Sport Fury Pace Car

For some reason, the Plymouth Sport Fury never aroused the excitement of other Chrysler muscle cars. It certainly had the great looks and could be ordered with all the top-drawer performance power plants. It never seemed to catch on, even with the exposure it got as the Indy Pace Car in 1965.

The model didn't get the attention of the performance-minded mostly because it was a heavier, full-size model. But getting all that national exposure in conjunction with Indy certainly didn't hurt.

The actual pace car carried the 426 Hemi, but the replicas that were built for the marketplace could be acquired with either the 383-cid or 318-cid power plants.

The Sport Fury was subtle compared with the performance models that followed. Bright white in color, the convertible had a light blue top.

Indy 500 lettering was printed on the rear quarters, but the largest lettering on the car was a blue "Plymouth" on the door. Chrysler Corporation never seemed to miss a chance to display either the Plymouth or Dodge names as prominently as possible. Above and below the Plymouth name were red letters "Official" and "Pace Car."

Plymouth also used the pace car as a publicity opportunity, in one of its earliest performance advertisements, to promote the performance implications of the model. The ad emphasized the 365-hp Hemi engine with its console-mounted tach, and Sure-Grip differential in the rear end.

The official 1965 Plymouth Fury Indy 500 Pace Car photo. (Indianapolis Motor Speedway Photo)

One of the 1965 Indy 500 Pace Cars today is a very interesting collectible.

The advertisement ended with words that implied a catchy racing image: “Put yourself in a Sport Fury soon. We’ll see you at the checkered flag.”

This flashy ’71 Dodge Challenger was that year’s Indy Pace Car, shown here at the Brickyard. (IMS Photo)

Plymouth’s national advertisement about the ’65 pace car, obviously photographed at the Brickyard. (Plymouth Advertisement)

1971 Dodge Challenger Pace Car

At a time when performance cars, including the Chrysler muscle machines, were facing the Clean Air Act, pressure from safety groups and spiraling insurance rates for performance cars were making hot cars a tough sell.

It came down to a situation that the Big Three manufacturers decided the Indy Pace Car program would be one of the fall guys. But local Indianapolis Dodge dealer Eldon Palmer, seeing great advertising potential, came to the rescue and agreed to provide 50 1971 Challenger convertibles for the “Brickyard” duties.

The actual pace car was a stock convertible, but due to the lack of factory sponsorship, funds didn’t allow any special engineering for the pacing duties. A Chrysler representative was scheduled to drive the car on race day, but was unable to attend due to illness. Palmer took on the driving duties.

The results were not the type of publicity that Palmer had hoped for as the Challenger smashed head-on into the photographers’ stand at the end of pit row. It happened when the Challenger was coming down pit row and the flag used to mark the starting line was hidden by crowds of people.

By the time Palmer realized he’d passed the starting line, it was too late. The car’s brakes faded and security guards waved him away from the track and into the stand. It was estimated the Challenger hit the stands at about 60 mph, causing several injuries. Fortunately, none of the injuries was fatal.

There are no serial numbers that define the pace car models, so it’s difficult to make a firm identification of these models. The cars at the track had flat hoods, Hemi Orange paint, white top, white interior, Goodyear raised white letter tires, and “Official Pace Car” decals on the doors and rear quarters. The “Dodge” name also was on the doors. All the lettering was done in white.

A number of other Dodge dealers apparently ordered a number of Hemi Orange convertibles from the factory with whatever options, engines, and transmissions they wanted. They put the Pace Car decals on later. The 318-cid, 340-cid, and 383-cid engines were available power plants.

The ’71 Challenger was painted Hemi Orange, one of the brightest pace cars ever to traverse historic Indy’s 2.5 miles.

Chapter Eleven: Mopar Racing Wins on Strip, Road, and Water

Mopar was very much alive on the quarter mile as well as the oval tracks. The Chrysler-built light Dodges and Plymouths were huge factor in the fast-growing popularity of drag racing.

Just as NASCAR success was advertised, so too were the exploits of Plymouth and Dodge on the quarter mile. Once again, the ultimate finish line was seeing new Chrysler products selling from dealer showrooms.

If the Hemi engines were big news over the hundreds of miles involved in NASCAR, they were a flashpoint for quarter mile racers. Their raw power housed inside light models like the Dodge Coronet and Demon and Plymouth´s Satellite and Barracuda helped make Chrysler king of the quarter mile.

Even the Plymouth Duster suggested drag racing as in "dust-off." In fact, one Duster-modified dragster during the period was called "Dusted."

Drag Racing

If you were a drag racing nut during the 1960s and ´70s, most likely Chrysler was at the head of your list.

Chrysler products were going like gangbusters, building pure race cars that went directly to race teams along with sponsoring a number of high-level teams. Never before, and probably never again, will this performance attitude exist.

Factory involvement with NHRA (the National Hot Rod Association) was encouraged—mostly due to the organization's definition of the term "stock." It all started with a group of young Chrysler engineers who formed a drag race team called "The Ramchargers." Believe it or not, it was done with the approval of

Jim Thornton and Herman Mozer (979) coming off the line in S/SA class.

Some days you win

Mozer and Al Eckstrand in final run for Top Stock Eliminator title.

Some days you lose

The Ramchargers team made their red-striped "Candymatic" Dodges famous burning up quarter miles in the 1960s and early ´70s. (OCW photo)

Chrysler management.

"The Ramchargers" became a legend with their dramatically-painted "B" body machines that featured red-and-white striping on the rear deck. There also was large "Ramcharger" lettering on the body sides.

During the mid-´60s, these were the cars to beat in national NHRA competition. Power under the hood was a blue-painted 426 Wedge engine set into an aluminum front end.

Dick Landy steered Dodges down the quarter mile and also was famous for his performance clinics at sponsoring Dodge dealers. (OCW photo)

Drag racing fans always thought of driver Roger Lindamood and his "Color Me Gone" dragsters. Here he´s winning with a Dodge. (OCW photo)

In 1964, a "Ramcharger Candymatic" Dodge took that year's NHRA Stock Eliminator crown.

Chrysler also used its 413-cid (and later 426-cid) Wedge engines in their early 1960s drag activities. Those models would be followed by the ultimate 426-cid Hemi engine.

Starting in the mid-1960s, Chrysler really set the drag world back with a series of lightweight, Hemi-powered models. Selected for this treatment were Dodge Coronets and Darts, along with Plymouth Belvederes and Barracudas.

The company squeezed by the assembly line rules with these cars. Basically, they were hand-built with lightweight sheet metal on the body and aluminum heads and magnesium intakes on the engines. Less weight was a key goal in the assembly of these cars.

The Chryslers did well in NHRA competition, specifically the new Super Stock Class, taking the title with ace mechanic and period superstar Bill "Grumpy" Jenkins at the wheel.

Small numbers were built in 1967 with just 55 each of the Dodge and Plymouth versions, namely the Coronet 440 S/S and Belvedere II S/S models. The

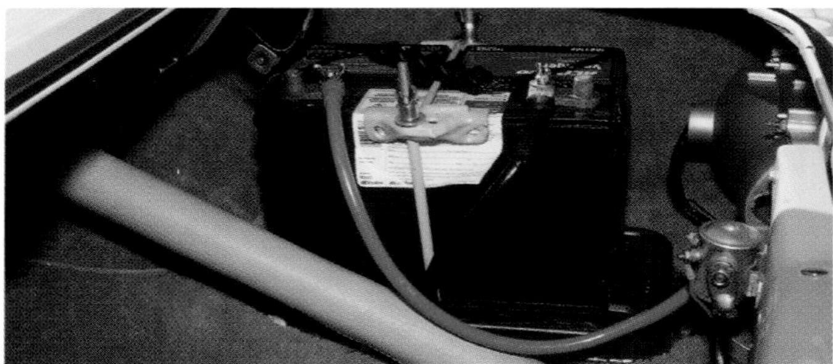

The trunk of a Ramcharger Super Stock car housed the battery—standard fair for these cars.

The highest possible horsepower figure was desired for the Ramcharger vehicles. They used an upgraded Hemi power plant.

This factory Super Stock ´66 Belvedere I was loaded with a 425 hp Hemi engine, 727 Torqueflite tranny, and 4.56 gearing.

special cars were identifiable from their VIN numbers. The Dodges started with WO23 and the Plymouths with RO23 prefixes.

In 1968, the final S/S year, there were 70 Barracuda S/S and 80 Dart S/S models built. VIN prefixes were BO29 for the Barracuda and LO23 for the Dart.

These awesome drag machines all had 426 Hemi engines and either four-speed or manually-shifted automatic transmissions. They were stripped to the hilt. Both radios and heaters were deleted. Their Hemi engine was a far cry from the street version. This Mopar mauler carried a hotter cam plus modified intake manifolds and carburetors.

It was an era when General Motors had dropped out of the racing business and the competition for Chrysler came down to a single Ford opponent with its awesome family of 427-cid engines.

Another direction also was taken by Chrysler on the drag scene during the 1960s, when a number of models were modified for the new NHRA FX (Factory Experimental) Class. The cars were greatly changed with their altered wheelbases. They became known as altered-wheelbase drag cars.

The modification, accomplished by a Detroit company called Amblewagon, reduced five inches from its 155-inch factory wheelbase.

The change was accomplished by moving the rear

The "One of 55" says it all. The large hood scoop on this ´67 Dodge Coronet Super Stock provided air to the Hemi engine. (Earl Brown Photo)

It wasn't easy to catch the Sox and Martin Barracuda on the strip or on film. It's shutting down all takers in 1970 action. (Hot Rod magazine photo)

The Dodge Coronet Super Stock carried this awesome twin-carbed Hemi powerplant. (Earl Brown Photo)

The factory Hemi Dart, built in limited numbers in 1968, carried this twin-carbed Hemi powerplant. (Muscle Car Restorations/John Balow Photo)

This 1968 Hemi Dart looks as good today at a Minneapolis area car show as is did when it came from Dodge. (Angelo Van Bogart/OCW)

A Mr. Norm's engine treatment was identified as a supercharged GSS. (Mike and Victoria Sylvester photo)

Mike and Victoria's Mr. Norm-prepared Dodge Demon carries the Grand Spaulding Dodge sticker on its rear deck. (Mike and Victoria Sylvester photo)

wheels forward 15 inches and moving the front wheels back five inches. The appearance was strange, to say the least. And when you came right down to it, these weird-looking machines really were the first "funny cars."

This Dodge Demon was prepared with the special Grand Spaulding Dodge touch by Mr. Norm Kraus and his crew. (Mike and Victoria Sylvester photo)

The wheel movements transferred additional weight to the rear, increasing traction for greater drag performance. That effectively provided a 50-50 weight balance. To fully achieve that goal, it also was necessary to accomplish considerable lightening in the frame and power train.

Initially, these creations weren't accepted by NHRA, but they got great attention with the rival AHRA (American Hot Rod Association) members and at unsanctioned appearances. The cars had top-gun drivers involved, with the likes of Ronnie Sox and Dick Landy. As these wild dragsters evolved, the characteristic factory hood scoop generally was discarded. Tall injection stacks sprouted through a hood slot.

Neither the Super Stock or FX cars were street legal and normally were purchased by race teams.

When it came to Chryslers and drag racing, there was an interesting operation connected with a Dodge dealership in Chicago, Illinois. It was known as Grand Spaulding Dodge and was located on West Grand Avenue in Chicago. Its famous radio slogan was "Often Imitated, Never Duplicated." It was owned and sponsored by its main man "Mr. Norm," Norm Kraus.

The dealership served drag racers with several functions. The first was with dealership upgrades to a number of Dodge models. If you wanted a performance boost for your Dodge, Mr. Norm was the man to see!

In 1968 and ´69, Chrysler would send him a regular Dart GTS 340 and he would perform all the necessary modifications to install a 440-cid engine in the car. Then, to identify it, Mr. Norm would take off the Chrysler "T" in the emblem, and put in a red "S." The final emblem had a silver G, a red S, and a silver S.

Mr. Norm and Grand Spaulding Dodge worked performance magic on the ´71 and ´72 GSS Demons, installing a Six-Pack induction system and custom air cleaner which upped their output to 300+ hp. The modifications were identified with custom "GSS Demon" stickers.

In 1972 and later, with the reduction in engine compression during the period, Mr. Norm turned to supercharging. A custom blower was set up for the Demon 340s. It was a popular model!

In addition to all the modifications, Mr. Norm also sponsored a top-gun drag racing effort. He was behind both the Super Stock and FX cars, all bearing the famous "Mr. Norm" name. He was often imitated but certainly never duplicated in the world of Chrysler car racing.

SCCA Trans Am Racing:Catching Up to the Circuit

Unlike its NASCAR racing experience, Chrysler got a late start in Trans Am racing. But it decided that late was better than not at all. One thing for sure, it hired a top-gun in Dan Gurney to be involved in the operation.

Engine displacement restrictions kept the team from using the powerful Hemis. With only 308 cubic inches allowed, it came down to destroking the existing 340-cid mill to 303.8 cid, with a single four-barrel carburetor.

Chrysler Corporation's famed engine builder Keith Black accomplished the build-up producing 450 hp.

The team, which also included young driver Swede Savage, began competition in 1970 in a pair of striking ´Cudas painted dark blue and wearing huge numbers 42 and 46.

A restored Dodge Challenger Trans Am shows the look it displayed during the golden era of American Trans Am racing. (SCCA photo)

The street version Challenger T/A SixPak looked top drawer with its body stripe, chin spoiler, and hood scoop.

They might have looked stock on the outside, but they were pure race car underneath. They weighed about 3,200 lbs. and used front torsion bars with rear parallel leaf springs.

An early publicity photo of the car showed the familiar AAR stripe cascading down the side of the car, interrupted by the number and Plymouth name.

The Trans Am series also showed two models with Plymouth's AAR ´Cuda and the Dodge Challenger T/A. The "AAR" stood for All-American Racers, a Sports Car Club of America racing group led by race veteran Dan Gurney. Challenger's T/A indicated the Trans Am Series sponsored by the SCCA.

In competition shots, the stripe was missing with

Challenger's T/A logo identified this model as the street version of the Dodge Trans Am racer.

The famous logo on the AAR ´Cuda (All-American Racing) was used on the street versions of the Trans Am-prepared race car.

The restored #48 Plymouth AAR ´Cuda, running in a vintage race, looks just as it did in its heyday. (SCCA photo)

only the Plymouth name on the front quarters and front spoiler.

Unfortunately, the team didn't meet its on-track expectations and the effort was disbanded following the season.

Shortly after the start of the Plymouth T/A effort, Dodge hustled together a team with Bob Tullius and Sam Posey as its pilots. They drove lime-green cars numbered 76 and 77. The only difference between this car and the AAR was the external sheet metal. The power train, suspension, and vehicle weights were identical in the Plymouth and Dodge cars.

The Dodge version looked much like the street version of the cars that still enjoy huge interest with 21st century collectors.

It carried a full-length body stripe with the Dodge name on the rear quarters. The large numerals were carried on the body sides. Unfortunately it, too, was gone after just one season.

Since a certain number of the AARs and Challenger T/As had to be built in order to compete in the Trans Am series, both auto divisions dressed up the externals to a high level. Both models used the same 340-cid power plant with three two-barrel carbs.

The AAR stood out then as it does now with that "Morse Code" racing stripe and the rear AAR emblem. The T/A used a flashy stripe that ended two-thirds of the way down the body with an embedded "T/A." Both models used the same triangular rear-deck spoiler.

Both the AAR and Challenger models were built in small numbers, with just 2,388 T/As and 2,724 AARs being constructed. They are the lone remembrance of the single-year Chrysler sponsored Trans Am effort.

Some of the most distinctive Chrysler-designed race looks came with the AAR ´Cuda and the Challenger T/A. Their exhaust extensions protruded just forward of the rear wheel opening and each carried functional lower front spoilers.

Dodge reportedly had planned to build a ´71 Challenger T/A, and actually may have built a few. The street version was to carry a 340-cid, four-barrel version instead of the Six Pack version used in the ´70 T/A model. Dodge backed out of racing for the 1971 season, and the model wasn't offered to the public.

Detailing of the Challenger T/A set it off as a Mopar fan favorite when new, a popularity it retains in the 21st century.

CHRYSLER'S RACE BOATS

During this period, Chrysler's famous engines also played heavily in national hydroplane racing. Not surprisingly, the Hemi power plant was a star on the water, just as it was on land.

In the early 1950s, the American Powerboat Association (APBA) formed the so-called Seven-Liter Class, which was about 427 cubic inches. The Hemi engine replaced the use of large truck and bus engines as it blew everybody away.

The powerful "Miss Desoto" was the seven-liter National Champion from 1957 through 1959, set a World Speed Record, and won the 1960 World Championship. Between 1962 and 1974, Hemi-powered seven-liter boats won National Championships 11 out of 13 years.

Another Hemi-powered seven-liter of the period, the "Miss Dodge Rebellion," was a two-time National Champion. In 1966, unlimited driver Bill Sterett devised an Unlimited Hydroplane powered by a pair of Hemi engines, a departure from the Allison and Merlin aircraft engines then in use.

The next year, Sterett's "Chrysler Crew" became the first automotive-engine-powered "Unlimited" to win a race. It hasn't happened since. One of the major contributors to that accomplishment was Keith Black, who today is a driving force in the design and development of follow-on Hemi derivative engines.

World Record Holder "Miss DeSoto" showed the company banner for that now-extinct car. The engine was a Chrysler built Wedge.

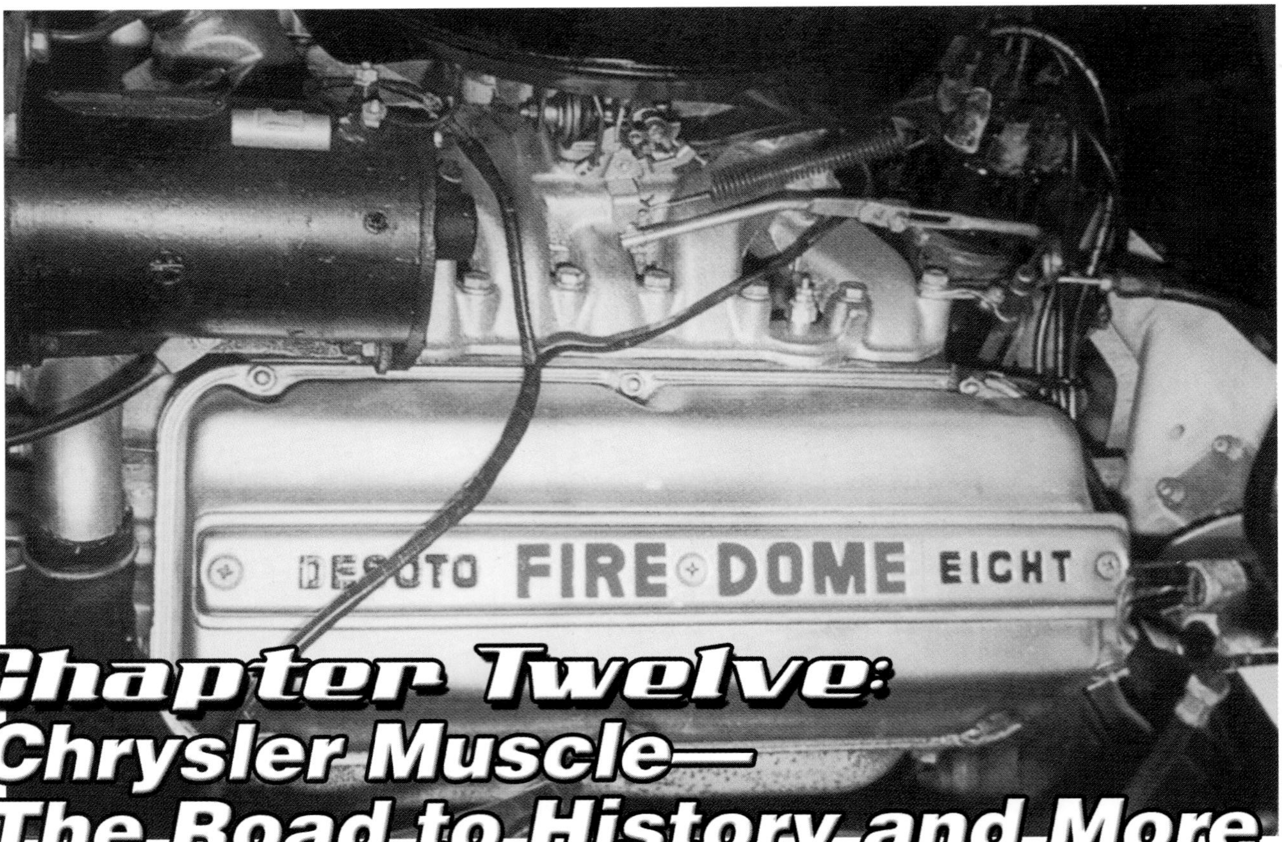

DeSoto Firedome V-8

Chapter Twelve: Chrysler Muscle— The Road to History and More

1950's: Chrysler 300s, V-8s — Predict Muscle

1955

1955 Chrysler C-300

1958

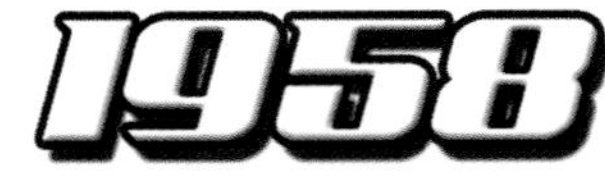

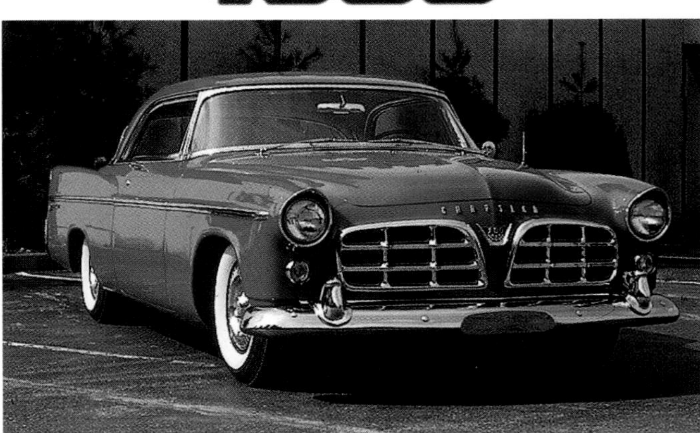

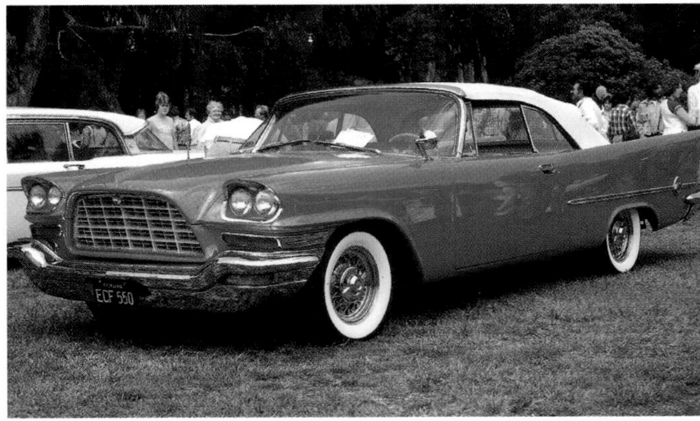

1958 Chrysler 300D

CHRYSLER's 300
Original Muscle Car

Amid the early mist of muscle car myths looms the image of the Chrysler 300. Meant for litheness rather than luxury, performance more than passenger amenities, the 300 dominated the muscle car trend and, seen now in an almost grandfatherly light, formed much of the trend itself as the movement developed. As such, it remains greatly honored today.

In 1955, the first 300 took to the streets. More than that, Chrysler moguls took it to the heights of stock car racing, which was strongly in vogue at that time. What made the first 300 hardtops so valiant on the track was stiff suspension and the marvelous Hemi V-8 engine that seemed beyond the limits of normal speed with its 300-horsepower punch. Hence, the model designation was a result of this, the most powerful American car produced that year.

Bob Rodger, chief engineer at Chrysler Division, worked with designer Virgil Exner to package raw power in a comely figure that appeared dashing, yet somewhat comfortable. After all, this was a passenger car concept with a touch of worldly authority. To be successful, it had to sell.

Chevrolet had recently pushed its performance model, the Corvette, to the forefront of showrooms. So had Ford with its Thunderbird. Kaiser's Darrin was yet another attempt at putting Mr. and Mrs. America in the single front seat of a sports car, albeit one of American design and handling. Nash-Healey had a European flair with American know-how, and Studebaker's European look had been transferred to its passenger car line. Now Chrysler stepped into the arena, but took the sporty image to an upscale size in keeping with the marque's tradition. Looking back, it was not far afield from what Buick was doing with its Skylark, what Packard was doing with its Caribbean, and what Cadillac was fielding with its Eldorado.

It was January of 1955 when the Chrysler 300 began production. First off was a white model, then a handful of red versions, and soon black became yet another color choice. That first 1955 model was labeled "C-300" for whatever reasons known internally, perhaps to connect the "C" of Chrysler to the horsepower rating. To have named it "A-300" could have conjured thoughts of Henry Ford's Model A, which was still a relatively fresh memory in the minds of car-buying Americans. To have prefixed it with the letter "A" might have also implied that the first such model had some teething to do before it cut loose with success. The "C" designation

In 1959, Chrysler slipped its 413-cid. wedge-head engine between the fenders of the 300E, replacing the Hemi-head engine that had been there since the car's 1955 creation.

was wise.

Buyers had to love hardtops to like the 300, since that was its only available body style. The hardtop trend had surfaced initially in early post-World War II production. By the early 1950s, it was being tried on nearly all makes. Properly executed, it afforded an element of sleek appearance due to a roofline that gracefully flowed in concert with body contours. It also served good use in two-tone colorations, the top being different than the body. That augmented the first-glance perception that what was coming down the road was a convertible rather than a hardtop. Yet, this model had all the convenience of a closed body as it offered more filtering of road noise, wind, and rain.

The model was grandly successful in grabbing attention for the corporate name and placed Chrysler ahead of the performance pack, even if the 300 was a fairly big car with its 126-inch wheelbase, which was utilized from 1955 through 1961. The car had a curb weight of 4,000 pounds for 1955, but the 331-cubic-inch V-8 Hemi moved it along well on the road and in sales with 1,725 units produced that year.

The Hemi-head engine offered 340 to 355 horsepower with 354-cubic-inch displacement for 1956; the numbers jumped to 392 cubic inches with 375 to 390 horsepower for 1957 and 1958. For 1959, the revered Hemi-head gave way to the wedge-head, which continued as the selected form through the 1965 letter models. The wedge-head V-8 was a whopping, gas-guzzling 413 cubic inches for 1959. Its peak horsepower year was 1962 when the block belted out 405 horsepower. For 1965, it was on the wane with 360 horsepower, yet still a very respectable figure that meant business.

Succeeding models generally gained weight, which meant all those pent-up horses had more to pull down the road. From its initial weight of 4,000 pounds for 1955, the 300 grew more girthful with 4,150 pounds for 1956, then 4,235 pounds for 1957 in hardtop form. The 1957 convertible scaled in at 4,390 pounds and must have brought dollar signs to the eyes of scrap dealers years later when the cars were towed into their yards. If "heavy" was your desire, the 1958 convertible beat them all at 4,475 pounds. For 1962 and 1963, the 300 went for weight loss, clinically dropping back to its original trim weight of 4,000 pounds for the hardtop. Lightest of all was the 1964 version at 3,965 pounds.

The 1960 300F took on unibody construction and had a simulated spare tire cover embedded in its trunk lid, almost as a visual throw-back to the days of the Lincoln Continental with its rear-mounted spare. Some buyers loved it. Others wondered. However it was seen in its day, the design motif remains memorable and still garners interesting comments at car shows.

What were some other styling features that marked the 300's advance? Fins took control of the rear on 1957 models and waned in the early 1960s, being fully tamed by 1963. Canted quad headlamps were integrated into the frontal design for 1961. Bodies looked longer and sleeker by the late 1950s. The 1963 and 1964 versions were relatively unique in Chrysler history and accounted for some of the best-running and

The 1956 Chrysler 300B was a screamer on the NASCAR tracks and local boulevards.

longest-lasting cars the corporation offered.

If rarity is your desire among hardtops, then consider a 1963 300J, which saw a 400-unit production, least of all the letter model 300's that were manufactured from 1955 through 1965. Next in rarity is the 1962 300H with 435 cars, then the 1959 300E with 618. Even in its final notable milestone year of 1965, there were 2,405 hardtops made.

The convertible version bowed for 1957 with 484 units that year. It dipped to 191 for 1958, then 140 for 1959. There were no convertible 300's in 1963, but the figure bounded to 625 for 1964 and carried 440 units for 1965.

The letter designation did not continue after 1965. The image had lost a high degree of luster and was more of a marketing tool than a symbol of pavement-sizzling performance.

Early versions up to 1962 are said to smack of custom-built quality construction. While 1963 through 1965 models are admirable, they have tended to lack the luster of earlier models. As with several other muscle car models by various makers, the market has jumped and plateaued now and then, based on supply and demand. Yet, the Chrysler 300 through 1965 remains a good buy.

As for an investment, don't get burned. Dealers in vintage cars know the market and how to smoke out buyers. Most car collectors don't. If you buy a 300 at an attractive figure and keep it well maintained for several years while enjoying its fabulous traits, you probably will do okay and may realize a respectable increase in your initial expenditure. But it is wise to buy the car because you like it rather than because you want an investment.

Value-wise, a 1955 300 tops the list of Chryslers at around $41,000, which is more than double the top value for a New Yorker sedan and about $5,000 more than a New Yorker convertible. The 1957 300C has reportedly sold for the top dollar of $44,000 as a hardtop and up to $53,000 for a convertible. For 1958 and 1959 models, the prices are comparable.

Highest on the list is the 1960 300F at $65,000 for the convertible, while the 1960 hardtop is around $53,000. A 1963 300J with the 413-cid. V-8 may set you back $31,000 in top shape.

Apparent bargains can be bought among later 300's. For 1964 through 1965, a four-door hardtop was added to the body range. Values run from $15,000 to $21,000, depending on convertible, two-door hardtop, or four-door configuration in these years. If the tendency holds, these cars will rise in value. Although they may not surpass the price tags of earlier 30´´s, they may still bring a worthy return. A 1964 300 convertible is still valued around $3,000 more than the New Yorker convertible.

Most 300's that you may encounter on the market will be of lesser quality than top-dollar survivors. Even so, experts say a 1960 300F in number 4 condition should range around $10,000 and the convertible around $13,000.

What can the milestone 300's from 1955 through 1965 offer collectors today? Outside of a Chrysler meet, they are generally uncommon and certainly turn heads. They represent the beachhead of activity for the muscle car craze. And they offer a pretty good ride with loads of power, at least as much as is legally allowed on city streets and roadways. Styling is distinctive and "period," plus you have a choice in 1950s-style design versus the 1960s.

Since they top the lists in Chrysler values throughout those years, they are prized as value leaders and cherished as "appreciators."

If you want an early muscle car, the mystique of a Chrysler 300 is very hard to match.

— *Gerald Pershbacher*

The 1960 Chrysler 300F was powered by a ram-inducted 413-cid V-8 that produced 375-hp. A 400-hp version was an available option.

1962-'63: Dawn of the Chrysler Muscle Cars

1962

1962 Dodge Dart 413 Ramcharger

1963

Chrysler "Max Wedge" engine

1963 Dodge 440 "Max Wedge"

1964: Selling Youth and Performance

GEORGE H. HURST

Hemi Under Glass Barracuda

The 1964 Dodge "Max Wedge"

The Chrysler Hemi racing engine

1965: Roaring into the Muscle Car Era

The "street" Hemi engine

1965 Plymouth Fury Indianapolis 500 Pace Car

1965

1965 Plymouth Satellite Convertible

1965 Dodge Hemi Coronet

1966:
The Dodge Charger

1966 Charger

1966 Charger

1966

1966 Charger

1967: Winnin' and Groovin'

One of the famed Petty #43 Plymouths

1967

Richard Petty and Plymouth dominate NASCAR

1967 Plymouth Belvedere GTX

1967 Dodge Coronet R/T

1968: Magical Mopars

1968 Plymouth Road Runner

1968 Dodge Charger R/T Hemi

1968 Dodge Charger R/T Hemi

1968

1968 Dodge Dart GTS 340

1968 Dodge Hemi Dart

1969: Ultimate Muscle

1969 Plymouth Road Runner

1969 Plymouth GTX

1969 Dodge Dart GTS

1969

1969 Dodge Charger Daytona

1969 Dodge Coronet 440 R/T

1969

1969 Dodge Charger R/T

1969 Dodge Hemi Charger

1970:
'Cudas, Wings and Psychedelic Things

1970 Plymouth Road Runner Superbird

1970 Plymouth Road Runner Superbird

1970

1970 Plymouth Duster 340

1970 Plymouth Hemi Barracuda

1970

1970 Plymouth ´Cuda AAR 340

1970 Dodge Dart Swinger

1970 Dodge Challenger T/A

1970 Road Runner 383

1970 Dodge Challenger

1971: Down the Muscle Car Highway

1971 Hemi ´Cuda

1971 Plymouth Hemi Road Runner

1971

1971 Plymouth Duster 340

1971 Dodge Charger Super Bee

1971 Dodge Challenger convertible

1971 Dodge Charger Super Bee 383

1971 Plymouth ´Cuda 383

1972 and Beyond

1972 Dodge Demon 340

1972 Dodge Challenger 340

1973

1973 Plymouth Duster

1974 Plymouth Road Runner

1974 Dodge Charger Magnum 440

1974 Plymouth ´Cuda

1974 Dodge Challenger 360

MOPAR FOREVER

1970 Plymouth Road Runner Superbird

Winged car reunion

Chapter Thirteen: Mopar Muscle Restored

This chapter is a special resource for those who cherish the Chrysler-built muscle cars. You'll find an array of information gathered by the authors.

For Mopar enthusiasts, authenticity often extends to getting the right paint code. During the late 1960s, Plymouth and Dodge often used the same color but the name was totally different—and the wilder the better!

Check out the color code charts from Dodge and Plymouth on these pages.

Clubs and registries are a way that car owners and car restorers can communicate to share information about every detail of their beloved Chrysler-Built products. This chapter also contains detailed lists of both clubs and registries.

A list of production figures of specific makes in the Mopar family has been tabulated and entered for your enjoyment here.

Today, Mopar Muscle lives on in creations that were need assembled more than 30 years after the original products were introduced. A new generation of Chrysler enthusiasts has fallen in love with these cars in their own special way. Some of the interpretations of the magical muscle machines can be found in this chapter.

This Challenger rips up the asphalt during the Chrysler Classic event competition.

If the early Dodge Coronet 440s strike your fancy, Chrysler Classic events usually have some excellent models to view.

Muscle Car Color Code Chart

Selected Colors from

PLYMOUTH

1966
(PP1) Bright Red
(661) Light Mauve Metallic
(KK1) Light Turquoise Metallic

1967
(EE1) Dark Blue Metallic
(PP1) Bright Blue Metallic
(ZZ1) Gold Metallic

1968
(RR1) Burgundy Metallic
(SS1) Sunfire Yellow
(FF1) Mist Green Metallic
(LL1) Surf Turquoise Metallic
(TT1) Avocado Green Metallic
(PP1) Matador Red
(QQ1) Bright (Electric) Blue Metallic
(Q5) Seafoam Turquoise
(EG5) Banana Yellow
(EK2) Vitamin C Orange
(Q5) Seafoam Turquoise Metallic
(R4) Performance Red
(T5) Bronze Fire Metallic
(EV2) Tor-Red
(Y2) Sunfire Yellow
(F3) Frost Green Metallic
(Y3) Yellow Gold
(F8) Seafoam Turquoise Metallic

1970
(FY1) Lemon Twist
(FC7) In Violet Metallic
(FJ5) Lime Green Metallic
(EF8) Ivy Green Metallic
(EK2) Vitamin C Orange
(FY1) Lemon Twist
(EV2) Tor-Red
(FY4) Citron Mist Metallic
(FE5) Rallye Red

1971
(EG5) Banana Yellow
(GB5) True Blue Metallic
(GY3) Curious Yellow
(FJ6) Green Go
(GY9) Tawny Gold Metallic
(FY1) Lemon Twist
(GY3) Citron Yellow

1971
(EK2) Vitamin C Orange
(GY8) Gold Leaf Metallic
(FC7) Plum Crazy
(GB5) True Blue Metallic
(FV6) Sassy Grass Green

1972
(FY1) Lemon Twist
(EV2) Tor-Red
(FE5) Rallye Red
(GY9) Tawny Gold Metallic
(GB5) True Blue Metallic
(GY8) Gold Leaf Metallic
(TB3) Basin Street Blue

**Not all colors available on all models*

A ´69 Daytona sports the ultra-rare Kelsey-Hayes slotted wheels—recalled shortly after they were issued.

Selected Colors from DODGE

1967
(881) Bright Blue Metallic
(EE1) Bright Red
(RR1) Yellow

1968
(QQ1) Bright Blue Metallic
(GG1) Racing Green Metallic
(SS1) Sunfire Yellow

1969
(EV2) Hemi Orange
(B5) Bright Blue Metallic
(Q5) Bright Turquoise Metallic
(T5) Copper Metallic

1970
(FJ5) Sublime
(FC7) Plum Crazy
(FK5) Dark Burnt Orange
(EK2) Go-Mango
(EB5) Bright Blue Metallic
(EV2) Hemi Orange
(FY1) Top Banana

1971
(EL5) Butterscotch
(B5) Bright Blue Metallic
(FJ6) Green Go
(FY1) Top Banana
(EV2) Hemi Orange
(FE5) Bright Red
(FC7) Plum Crazy
(GY3) Citron Yella

1972
(EV2) Hemi Orange
(FE5) Bright Red
(GB3) Super Blue
(FY1) Top Banana
(TB3) Super Blue

** Not all colors were available with all models*

Many stock-appearing Mopars still get into the drag racing scene. This Super Bee awaits its turn for a 1,320 foot run.

A covey of AAR 'Cudas show their stuff at a recent Mopar Nationals event.

Black is used to set off the grille area on this ´69 Dodge Charger.

The use of black is seen on the air cleaner cover of this 440-cid engine in a ´70 Challenger.

Registries

1. **1969 GTX Registry**
   38 Crossbow Road, Grayson, KY 41143
2. **69-1/2 440 Six Pack/440+6bbl Registry**
   PO Box 52044, Dover, DE 19902-0106
3. **AAR ´Cuda Registry**
   861 Kent Street, Portland, MI 48875
4. **Challenger T/A Registry**
   PO Box 9632, Ketchikan, AK 99901
5. **Classic ´60s and ´70s Mopar Registry**
   19F Aggie Village, Logan, UT 84322
6. **Dart 1967 and 1968 GTS Registry**
   1484 Pioneer Drive, Cedar City, UT 84720
7. **Dart 1969 GTS Registry**
   1041 Churchill Drive, Bolingbrook, IL 60439
8. **1970 Dart Swinger 340 Registry**
   Dartsclub@snet.net
9. **Dodge Challenger Registry**
   10 Tarra Drive, New Castle, DE 19720
10. **Dodge Charger Registry**
    109 Carver Place, Grafton, VA 23692
11. **Formula S Registry**
    PO Box 161, Pine Valley, CA 91962
12. **Super Bee Registry**
    39831 Pinebrook, Sterling Heights, MI 45310
13. **´67-´68 GTS Registry**
    4784 Pioneer Drive, Cedar City, UT 84720
14. **1970-´71 Plymouth and Dodge E-Body Convertible Registry**
    CUDAIZED@concentric.net
15. **1969-´70 ModTop Registry for Plymouths and Dodges**
    www.public.usit.net/jmoore/modregistry.html
16. **Plymouth Valiant Registry**
    2121 Seaport Circle, Winter Park, FL 32792

Clubs

1. **273 Power Pack Dart Owners Club**
   PO Box 867, Richboro, PA 18954
2. **Plymouth Valiant Club**
   2121 Seaport Circle, Winter Park, FL 32792
3. **Birds´n Bees Foundation**
   1860 Faye Rd., Akron, OH 44306
4. **Big Block Barracuda/Dart Association**
   614 Railway Road, Grafton, VA 23692
5. **Rapid Transit System Club**
   1513 South 121st St., Omaha, NE 68144
6. **Darts (aka The Darts Club)**
   Dartsclub@snet.net
7. **Chrysler R/T Club**
   PO Box 16421, Portland, OR 97216
8. **Daytona/Superbird Auto Show**
   13717 W. Green Meadows Drive, New Berlin, WI 53151
9. **Dodge Brothers Club**
   4 Window Street, Milford, NH 03035
10. **Early Hemi Assn.**
    233 Rogue River Highway #354, Grants Pass, OR 97527
11. **Max Wedge Owners Assn.**
    12661 Silver Fox Road, Los Calamitous, CA 90720
12. **Mopar Club USA**
    PO Box 1445, Massapequa, NY 11758

13. Mopar Magic Unlimited
PO Box 52061, Shreveport, LA 71135

14. Mopar Muscle International
879 Summaries Avenue, Washington, PA 15301

15. Mopar Power Club
218 N. Kentucky Avenue, Massapequa, NY 11758

16. Mopar Rapid Transit Club
392 Hillside Drive, China Grove, NC 28023

17. National Chrysler Products Club
317 South Jackson St., Strasburg, PA 17579

18. National F-Body Owners Assn.
PO Box 1348, Popular Bluff, MO 63901

19. National Hemi Owners Association
1593 South Reese, Reese, MI 48757

20. Plymouth Barracuda/'Cuda Owners Assn.
4825 Indian Trail Rd., Northampton, PA 15067

21. Plymouth Owners Club
PO Box 345, Walhalla, ND 58282

Even rare winged cars come out in force at the Mopar Nats. There is awesome competition at the car show event.

The Johnny Lightning Company is producing a number of Mopar diecast models, shown here are Road Runner and Daytona models.

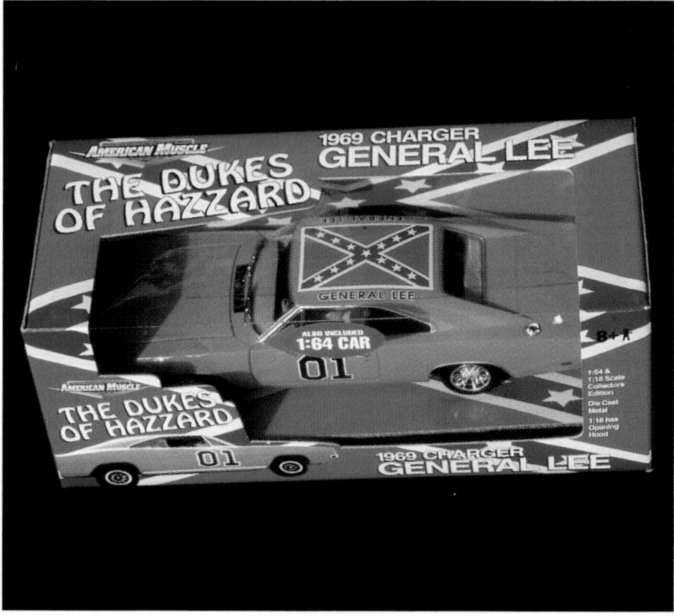

Even new diecast models of the "General Lee" are still being produced. One of the best is by American Muscle.

This miniature gallery of vintage Mopar powerplants come in plastic kit form from Gibson Engines. (Gibson Engines Photo)

Vintage Mopar lives on thanks to three popular magazines: Mopar Collectors Guide, Mopar Muscle, *and* Mopar Action.

Collector Ken Schrader's '69 Charger was stolen and stripped before it was recovered and restored, an ordeal that took patience.

From this tough stance, you know this ´69 GTS is one tough performance machine.

Larry Gordon found this ´70 Challenger R/T beaten and stomped flat. Amazingly, he restored it to this pristine level.

Those outlandish colors! They're typified by the Lime Green metallic '70 'Cuda. The rainbow of Chrysler colors stood out!

Home of a Chrysler plant for many years, it's a sea of muscle and wild colors at the annual New Castle, Indiana, gathering of the Mopar faithful.

Chrysler Muscle Car Production (ALL V-8's)

	DODGE		PLYMOUTH	
1965			Barracuda	41,601
1966			Barracuda	25,536
1967	Coronet	10,181	Barracuda	41,846
			GTX	12,115
1968	GTS Dart	8,102	Barracuda	29,254
	Coronet R/T	10,558	GTX	18,272
	Super Bee	7,842	Road Runner	44,598
	Charger R/T	17,665		
1969	GTS Dart	6,077	Barracuda	20,626
	Coronet R/T	6,955	GTX	15,010
	Super Bee	26,125	Road Runner	82,109
	Charger	64,837		
	Daytona	503		
	Charger 500	500		
	Charger R/T	9,298		
1970	Chall. R/T	14,759	Barracuda	21,208
	Chall. T/A	2,399	AAR Cuda	2,724
	Super Bee	1,254	GTX	7,202
	Coronet R/T	2,400	Road Runner	39,110
1971	Dart Demon	7,899	Barracuda	15,866
	Chall. R/T	3,814	´Cuda	293
	Charger R/T	2,659	GTX	2,626
	Super Bee	4,144	Duster 340	403
			Road Runner	13,046
1972	Dart Demon 340	8,739	Barracuda	8,951
	Chall. Ralleye	6,902	´Cuda	6,382
			Road Runner	6,831
			Duster 340	14,132

Chrysler Modified Muscle

Recent Sightings

A high-powered Dodge Dart dragster sports a supercharger to pump up its performance. Its stock body wears a sensational paint scheme.

"The Purple Gang" '70 Cuda dragster carries big pony power to pump up performance.

The "High Adventure Hemi" is based on a 1963 Plymouth. It announces to everyone that it carries Chrysler's famed 426 power plant under the hood.

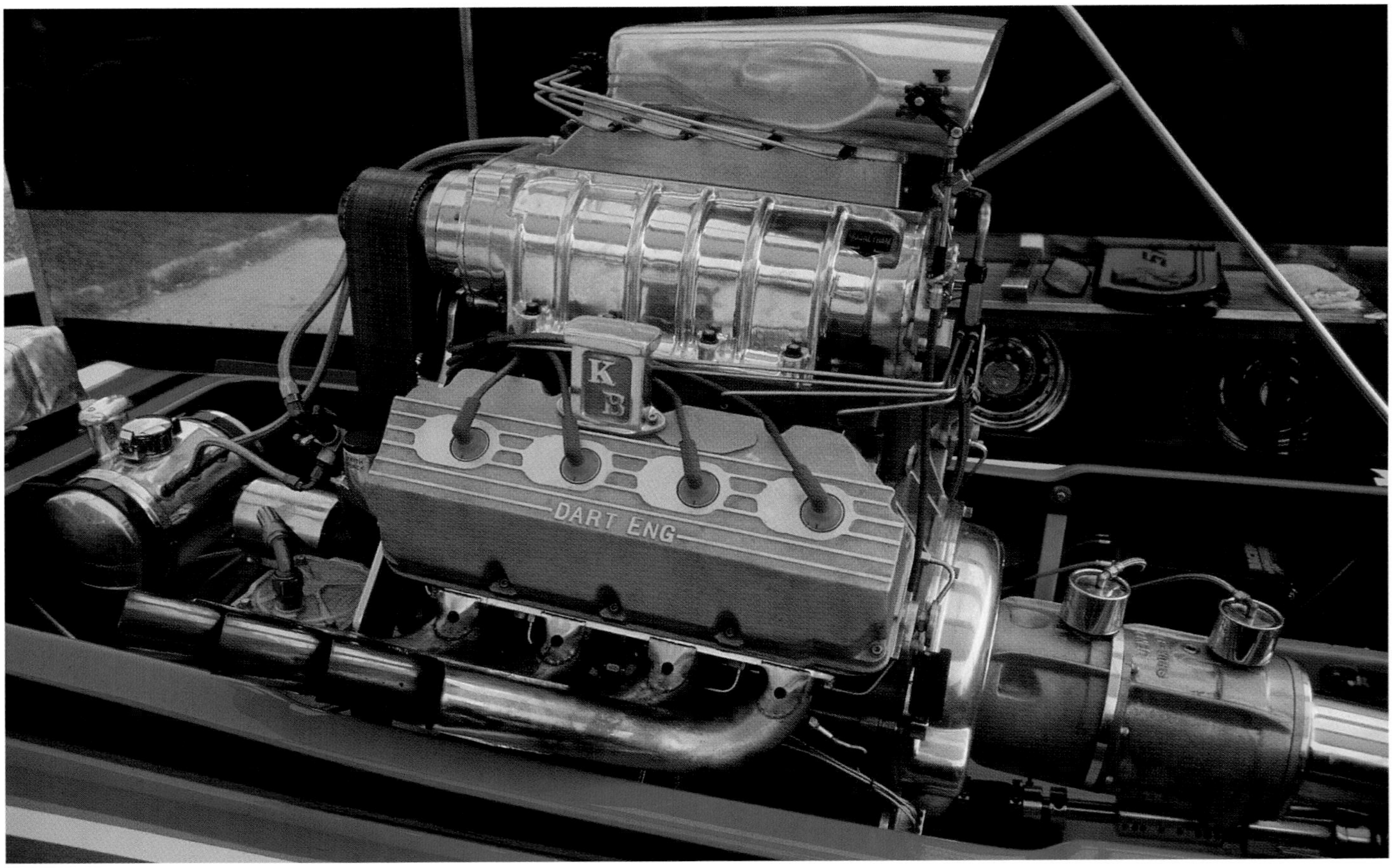

Advanced versions of the Hemi engine are still racing. A Top Fuel drag boat uses a supercharged Hemi to power down its liquid quarter mile.

Here's one person's interpretation of a modern dream machine based on an early 1970s E-body Chrysler car.

Guys and gals prepare to drag their nearly-stock Mopars at a modern drag strip's staging area.

The stripe is vintage stock but the displacement is not. The owner inserted the displacement of his modified engine.

Many vintage Mopar dragsters use engines that are a combination of the old and the new.

Chapter Fourteen: Musclecarus Rapidus Moparum Translating the Muscle

"A" body
The body style of the smallest Chrysler muscle cars—the Duster, Demon, and Dart.

AAR ´Cuda
Spruced-up version of the ´Cuda that enabled qualification for the SCCA Trans Am racing series.

Altered wheelbase
Wheelbase-modified '60s drag cars, also known as "altereds."

ARCA
The Automobile Racing Club of America, based in Toledo, Ohio.

"B" body
The body style used by the most popular Chrysler-produced muscle cars including the Road Runner, Super Bee, and Charger.

Barracuda
Early Plymouth, originally known for its sloping glass rear window, This Chrysler model lasted through the entire "muscle car" era.

"Beep-beep"
The unique sound of the Plymouth Road Runner's horn which replicated the signature call of the Warner Brothers cartoon character.

Bullitt
Famous 1968 Steve McQueen movie that co-starred a black ´68 Charger R/T in one of the most famous chase scenes ever filmed.

Candymatic
A red-striped paint scheme made popular by the famed "Ramcharger" dragster teams of the 1960s.

Centron Yellow
A 1970 Dodge color.

Challenger
A Dodge performance model that enjoyed great popularity from its classic body styling.

Charger
Probably the most-famous Dodge model. Identified by its slanted roof, it was a bare-bones muscle machine.

Chrysler Classic Events
Six annual events that highlight the vintage Chrysler muscle cars.

Chrysler 300
A family of luxury-performance cars with large V-8s that many consider to be the first muscle cars.

Coke bottle
Curved styling introduced in the slope-backed '66 Dodge Charger that later predicted the early Dodge and Plymouth muscle car look.

Commando
Plymouth name for certain high-performance engines.

Coronet
A Dodge line that carried the same performance equipment as Chrysler models but didn't get the attention or popularity.

Cragar mags
A popular after-market wheel used on Dodge and Plymouth muscle cars.

'Cuda
Nickname for Chrysler's Barracuda eventually used on performance models.

Curious Yellow
A 1971 Plymouth color and also a name of a ´60s movie.

Dart
Dodge version of the smallest Chrysler muscle models.

Daytona
The wild-and-crazy winged version of the Dodge Charger that was built specifically to qualify for NASCAR racing.

Demon
Stylish version of the Dodge Dart which appeared in the early 1970s.

Dodge Fever
Edgy 1960s ad campaign that introduced a new generation of Dodges led by their spectacular muscle cars.

Dodge Rebellion
The mid-´60s Dodge advertising campaign that heralded a performance and youth era for Dodge.

Check out the chrome-endowed engine compartment of this ´70 Road Runner. Be sure to shield your eyes!

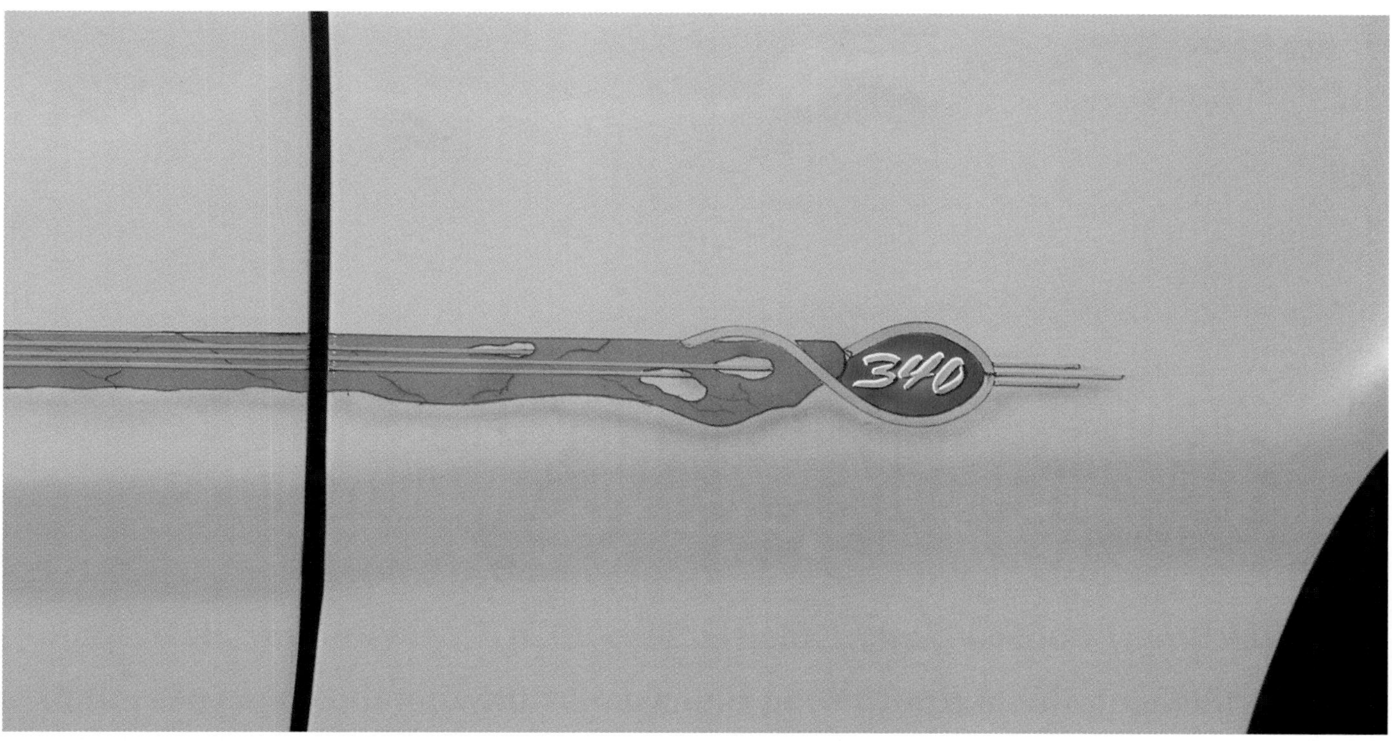

The owner of this vintage Duster decided to pep up the side trim. It looks pretty snazzy!

The Hemi engine never looked this good in factory trim. This Hemi's drag engine is adorned with twin carbs, a tunnel-ram intake and lots of chrome.

Duster
Plymouth's version of the smallest Chrysler muscle cars.

"E" body
The body style code used for Dodge Challenger and Plymouth 'Cuda models.

General Lee
A group of modified Hemi Orange '69 Chargers used in the *Dukes of Hazzard* TV show.

Go Mango
A 1970 Dodge color.

Grabber
A hood scoop lid, available on cars with Chrysler 440 cid and Hemi engines that opened to take in air. Decorated with a cartoon character.

Bob Morgan converted his '72 'Cuda into a magnificent show car. The rear end is out-of-sight on this totally detailed car!

A gorgeous, modified 1971 Road Runner.

Green Go
A 1971 Dodge color.

GTX
Luxury version of Plymouth Belvedere. Lasted from 1967 through 1971.

Hang 10
Unique surfing-inspired version of Dodge Dart in 1974-'75. It was listed as Dodge's option code A63.

Hemi engine
Most popular high-performance engine ever built. Used in all Chrysler models, especially the Dodge and Plymouth lines.

Hemi Orange
One of the most popular colors used during the Chrysler performance era. Also used on engine blocks.

Homologation
An approval process. NASCAR had to set production standards with Chrysler in order to approve the Plymouth Road Runner Superbird and Dodge Charger Daytona for racing.

IMCA
The International Motor Contest Association, a venerable grassroots motor racing association based in Vinton, Iowa.

In violet
The FC7 code used by Plymouth and the same color as Dodge's Plum Crazy.

Lemon Twist
Popular Plymouth color.

Magnum
Dodge engine prefix, ie, a 440 Magnum engine.

This Charger carries a classy side stripe that includes its name carried within.

Phoenix Graphix of Tempe, Arizona, makes vintage Plymouth and Dodge decals—totally correct for your ´60s and ´70s Mopar.

Miss DeSoto
A Hemi-powered racing boat that was national champion from 1957-'59.

Mr. Norm
Chicago's Norm Kraus, who was famous for modifying Dodges at his Grand Spaulding Dodge dealership.

Modified
A drag racing class.

MOPAR
The historic Chrysler Division (and current Daimler Chrysler arm) that provides parts and services for maintenance, performance, and vehicle care. Also used as a popular nickname for Chrysler cars, especially in the muscle car era.

MOPAR Nationals
The largest collection of vintage Dodge/Plymouth muscle cars. An event that gathers annually at National Trail Raceway near Columbus, Ohio.

Morse code stripe
The striking interrupted body stripe used on the 1970 AAR 'Cuda.

Mopar events across the country provide a supply of vintage sheet metal parts.

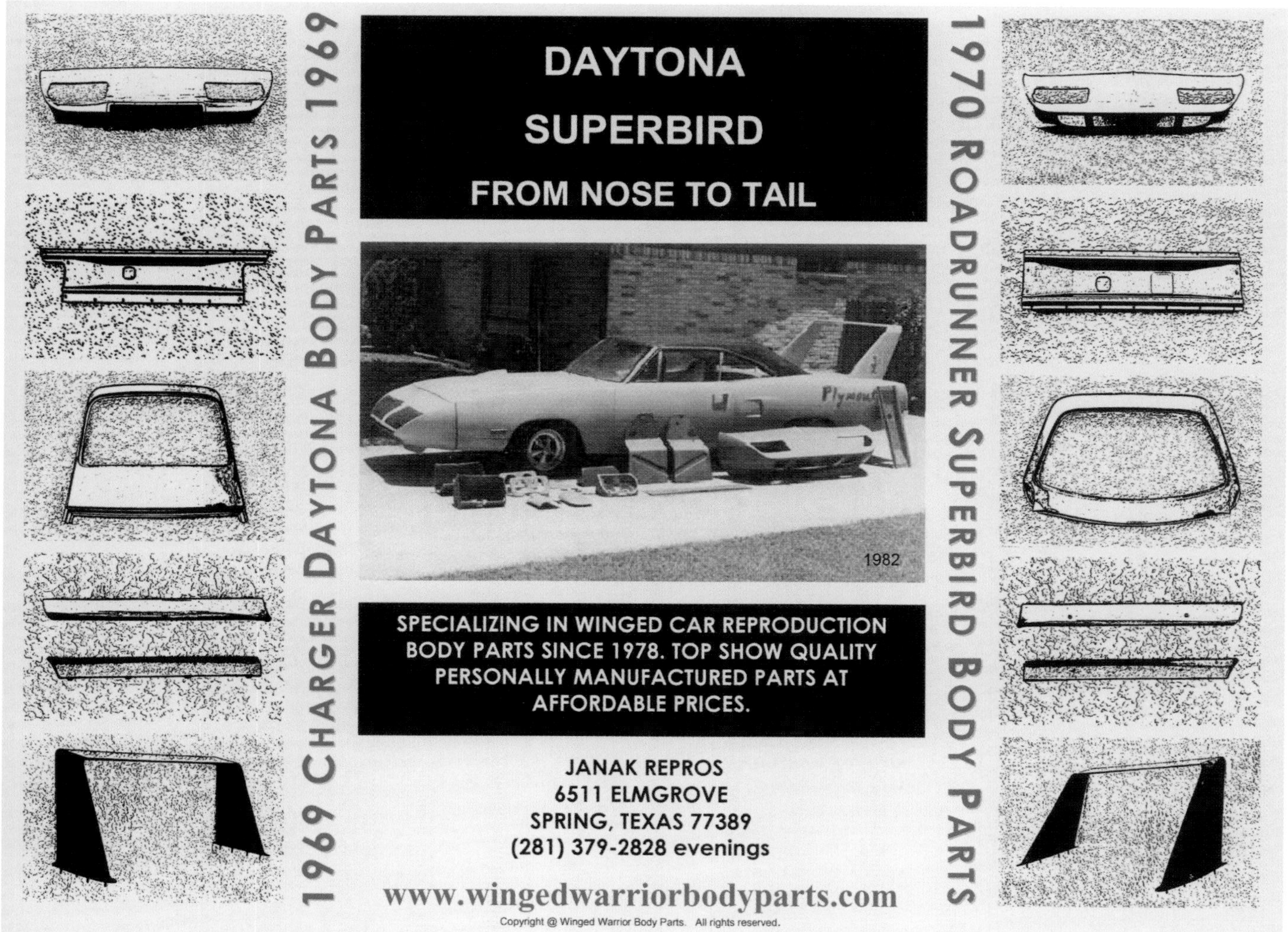

Janak Repros, Spring, Texas, provides accurate parts to convert your Charger or Road Runner into a winged warrior. The finished product is hard to detect from the original. (Janak Repros Advertisement)

Panther Pink
Outlandish Dodge color in 1970 and ´71.

Petty, Richard
Legendary NASCAR driver who used both Dodge and Plymouth race cars.

Power bulge
The distinctive look of the Plymouth Road Runner hood suggesting the power that lay beneath.

Psychedelic
Wild color schemes of the late ´60s introduced in the teen culture and brought into the mainstream by advertisers, car makers, and manufacturers.

R/T
Performance and appearance option package. Most times mentioned as standing for Road-and-Track.

Ramchargers
Chrysler Corporation employees who formed a successful drag racing team of the early to mid ´60s.

Rapid Transit Authority
Nickname for Plymouth's muscle car inventory which began being used in 1970 advertising and promotions.

Road Runner
Probably the most popular Plymouth muscle version. Produced from 1969 through the muscle era and beyond.

SE Option
Dodge appearance option during the 1970s.

Scat Pack
Dodge nickname for its muscle car fleet.

Shaker hood
Chrysler called this air intake device the "Incredible Quivering Exposed Cold Air Grabber." It was popularly called the "Shaker hood" and could be controlled by the driver.

Six-Barrel
Plymouth's designation for its three Holley two-barrel carburetion system.

Bob Morman's Mopar collection includes a room full of winged Daytonas and SuperBirds and a '71 Challenger Indy Pace Car.

Six-Pack
Dodge's designation for the same three two-barrel carburetion system.

Six Pak
The exterior identification used for 1970 Dodge Challengers with the "Six Pack" carburetion system.

Sox and Martin
Famous 1960s drag race team who used Chrysler products.

Sublime
1970 Dodge version of lime green.

Sunfire Yellow
1969 Dodge shade of yellow.

Super Bee
A performance model of the Dodge Charger that featured a cartoon bee mascot.

Super Stock
A family of specially-built, lightweight cars, strictly for drag racing.

Swinger
The Dodge Dart-based two-door hardtop featured a 340-cid V-8 and the promise of a muscle car for the budget-minded.

Top Banana
A 1972 Dodge color choice.

TorqueFlite automatic
The rugged and smooth transmission was the perfect mate for delivering the performance goods of the Chrysler muscle car engines.

Tor-red
Plymouth's EV2 color choice that was really a popular shade of orange.

Vitamin C orange
A Plymouth color offered from 1969 through 1971.

W23 wheel
A structurally flawed Kelsey-Hayes slotted wheel originally used on the '69 Charger Daytona. It was recalled by Chrysler. Originals now are collected.

Wedge engines
A family of Chrysler high-performance engines in the early 1960s which used wedge-shaped combustion chambers and came in 413- and 426-cid form.

Winged warriors
The limited production ´69 Dodge Charger Daytona and ´70 Plymouth Road Runner Superbird were designed for heavily competitive NASCAR racing. Their aerodynamic noses and huge spoilers made them both aerodynamic and controversial.

Bob Morman, Peebles, Ohio, is a long-time Mopar dealer who still loves the cars. Here is his replica ´73-´74 Petty Dodge.

Bill Holder

An automotive writer for more than 25 years, Bill Holder has published hundreds of articles for magazines such as *MOPAR Muscle*, *Muscle Car Review*, and *MOPAR Collectors Guide*. In addition, he has written for such publications as *Mustang Monthly* and *Super Ford*.

Bill also has written several books with a specific emphasis on the muscle car era.

A retired aerospace engineer, Bill also has written more than 50 books on military aircraft, stock cars, and open-wheel racing.

He is a regular attendee at Chrysler Classic events and the MOPAR Nationals. Bill lives in Riverside, Ohio.

Phil Kunz

Professional photojournalist Phil Kunz has seen his works published in many racing and automotive books and magazines.

His assignments have included photographing boat racing as well as various auto racing vehicles and muscle cars.

Phil's quality photos have appeared in countless works and in various publications.

A Kettering, Ohio, resident, Phil has experience as both a hydroplane racer and owner. He was a founder of the Mid American Championship Hydroplane (M.A.C.H.) sanctioning organization.

He has collaborated with writer Bill Holder on various projects over the last 18 years.